PRAISE FOR *CULTURE FIRST CLASSROOMS*

This book is a true game changer, especially in today's education climate. Giving educators an authentic voice is vital, and equipping them with strategies to effectively meet the needs of students starts with the kind of leadership presented in this book. Together, Darrin and Katie bring a unique perspective and beautifully craft their message through stories and case studies all educators would benefit from reading. It is relatable and inspiring, serving up messages of hope. Most importantly, it reminds us that nurturing relationships is the cornerstone of a "culture first classroom" and thriving school system. I highly recommend this book to anyone who needs a boost in morale and new ideas to implement in their own practice. Well done!

Charlie Peck
Keynote Speaker | Author | School Mental Health Consultant

Culture First Classrooms is an inspiring, accessible read for educators at all levels. Its structure makes it easy to absorb valuable insights effortlessly. With short, digestible chapters, reflection questions, and real stories from contributors nationwide, the book feels authentic and actionable. I especially appreciated the shift from compliance to engagement and the essential chapter on trauma sensitivity. The clear action steps after each chapter ensure immediate application. This book doesn't just discuss positive school culture–it guides you there. Highly recommended!

Ginger Healy
LCSW | School Therapist | Author
Program Director for the Attachment & Trauma Network

This book is a must read for anyone in education. Have you ever wished that someone would travel all over the country and gather wisdom from some of the best educators in the world? That's what this book is: A wealth of information from the people who are making a difference for kids everyday. Thank you, Darrin and Katie, for making sharing this wealth of information.

Josh Varner
Speaker | Author | Consultant

As someone who believes deeply in the power of culture to transform learning, *Culture First Classrooms* truly resonated with me. Dr. Darrin Peppard and Katie Kinder don't just talk about what makes a great school—they show us how to build one, starting with the heart of every classroom. Their message is clear: Culture isn't something that happens by chance; it's something we create with intention. Through powerful stories, strategies, and insights from passionate educators, they remind us that leadership and relationships are at the core of every thriving school. I especially love their emphasis on celebrating the wins, supporting each other, and finding joy in this important work. If you're ready to lead with heart and purpose, read this!

Kim Strobel
Keynote Speaker | Author of Teach Happy *| CEO of Strobel Education*

When I first sat down to read *Culture First Classrooms*, I planned to spend a few minutes reading the first section before moving on to my list of tasks for the day. However, I was so intrigued that I couldn't put it down! I love the way Darrin and Katie have provided actionable steps to try out the strategies in the book. It's a delightful read and having the opportunity to hear from so many inspirational educational leaders at once makes this book even better. I enjoyed gathering lesson ideas (Hello, toothpaste!) and reflecting on how the design of my classroom can impact students. I came away with so many ways to consider the culture first and leave a lasting impression on students. Bravo!

Hilary Statum
Teacher | Author | National Presenter

If you're an educator looking to transform your classroom into a thriving, engaging, and culture-first space, *Culture First Classrooms* is a must-read! Dr. Darrin Peppard and Katie Kinder bring real, practical strategies that you can implement immediately–because let's be real, educators don't have time for fluff. This book is packed with heart, humor, and wisdom from educators who walk the talk. It reminds us that the magic in education isn't just in lesson plans–it's in leadership, relationships, and the culture we intentionally create. A game-changer for teachers and leaders alike!

Dr. Donya Ball
Superintendent | Speaker | Author

Building a strong school culture doesn't happen by accident, it takes intentional leadership, real relationships, and practical strategies. In *Culture First Classrooms*, Dr. Darrin Peppard and Katie Kinder deliver all three, offering insights educators can apply immediately. As an educational culture and climate expert, I know firsthand the power of this work. I also value fresh perspectives. This book is another powerful resource for educators looking to transform their schools. Read it, apply it, and most importantly, put culture first.

"Stand Tall" Steve Bollar
Educational Culture & Climate Expert | Speaker | Author of Just Do This…

Culture First Classrooms provides the inspiration every educator needs, whether you've been teaching for 5 days or 50 years. The numerous illustrative stories shared by experienced educators reminds us that classroom management is only possible if our learning spaces are welcoming, respectful, and supportive of all learners.

Crystal Frommert
Educator | Author of When Calling Parents isn't Your Calling

Dr. Darrin Peppard and Katie Kinder have written a book that gives great insight into what it takes to lead and to teach. The book features different leaders and teachers all with different styles and ideas to become stronger in their craft. *Culture First Classrooms* is a great resource for educators interested in becoming their best self.

Kim Campbell
Proud Middle School Teacher | Daring Dean of Students | Crazy Consultant

You can have really great programs and curriculum, but without relationships and leadership, you can only take all of that so far. In *Culture First Classrooms,* by Katie Kinder and Darrin Peppard, you're getting practical and attainable ideas to build culture that lasts and makes an impact for kids, staff and the community. Relationships matter most and you're going to enjoy *Culture First Classrooms,* but more importantly, you're going to learn, grow and have a game plan to do it all in your school as well!

Adam Welcome
Educator | Author | Speaker

At a time when education feels unpredictable and overwhelming, this book is a powerful reminder that the best educators focus on what they can control. With wisdom, warmth, and practical guidance, Katie and Darrin provide a roadmap for creating a classroom where students feel safe, seen, and motivated. From building strong relationships and setting clear expectations to designing a supportive learning environment, this book equips teachers with strategies that foster both academic and personal success. More than a guide, it's a call to lead with love, compassion, and an unshakable belief in every child's potential.

Julie Schmidt Hasson
Professor | Researcher | Resilience Trainer

One of the best things is how the book leaves you feeling both informed and inspired. Darrin and Katie emphasize that the path of education is anything but easy, and by highlighting the voices of those who are actively navigating these challenges, it reassures educators that they are not alone. This sense of camaraderie is valuable for maintaining morale, while also providing tangible tools that can improve individual teaching practices and school-wide initiatives. Through my reading I was reminded that while the journey of an educator is demanding, it's also filled with opportunities for growth, connection, and positive change. We will never find a greater calling than what we do every day, and reading this book told me to keep going!

Bentli Lewis
Principal, Oakbrook Middle School

Culture First Classrooms is a must-read for educators looking to transform their schools from the inside out. Darrin Peppard and Katie Kinder expertly blend leadership, relationships, and practical strategies to create classrooms where culture is the foundation of student success. This book is packed with insights, real-world experiences, and actionable steps that empower educators to build meaningful connections, foster trust, and create learning environments where both students and teachers thrive. If you're ready to put culture at the heart of your school, this book is your roadmap!

Joshua Stamper
Educator | Speaker, |Author | Podcaster

Seeking input and voice from those that are still in the arena make this a unique stand out book. The authenticity and honesty of *Culture First Classrooms* makes it a must read. Darrin Peppard is a leading voice in 2025, and his work is a must for any educational leader.

Todd Bloomer
Author | Speaker | Leader

Culture First Classrooms is a game-changer for educators who want to build strong, positive environments where both students and staff thrive. The blend of real-world stories from 23 incredible educators and practical, actionable strategies makes this book an absolute must-read for anyone serious about transforming school culture. Darrin Peppard and Katie Kinder's passion for putting culture first shines through on every page!

Jonathan Alsheimer
Educator | Author | Speaker

CULTURE FIRST
CLASSROOMS

LEADERSHIP, RELATIONSHIPS, AND PRACTICES THAT TRANSFORM SCHOOLS

DARRIN PEPPARD
KATIE KINDER

Culture First Classrooms: Leadership, Relationships, and Practices that Transform Classrooms

Copyright © by Darrin Peppard and Katie Kinder
First Edition 2025

All rights reserved.

No part of this publication may be reproduced in any form, or by any means, electronic or mechanical, including photocopying, recording, or any information browsing, storage or retrieval system, without permission in writing from the publisher.

Road to Awesome, LLC.

Being an educator is a tough job, always has been. Everyone's an expert simply because they went to school, and most are happy to tell you how it should be done. But you keep going, even when it's hard, because you love what you do and the young people you get to work with.

Whether you're a 30-year veteran or a brand new baby teacher, thank you for what you do every single day. Darrin and Katie dedicate this book to you, the educator who just keeps showing up!

TABLE OF CONTENTS

Introduction	1
Chapter One More Than Just Classroom Management	9
Chapter Two A Tale of Two Superintendents	15
Chapter Three Leadership that Shapes Culture	25
Chapter Four Relationships as the Heart of Culture	55
Chapter Five Inclusive and Intentional Environments	85
Chapter Six Student-Centered Practices that Engage	107
Chapter Seven Trauma-Informed Practices for Healing and Growth	139
Chapter Eight Building a Culture of Community	173
Chapter Nine Accountability, Growth, and Legacy	201
Conclusion	233
About the Author	243

Introduction

We talk all the time about what matters in schools. Everyone seems to have an opinion - just open your social media. But the reality is this: if you want to make a difference in the life of a child, you have to touch their heart. As Katie and I set out to write this book, we had no idea what we intended to put together. We knew that we wanted to impact you and your classrooms and schools, but weren't sure what this book would be specifically focused on. Over time, with the people we were fortunate enough to meet and are blessed to work with in schools across North America, we have unlocked the obvious truth: Culture matters. (Duh, right?) But how often do we stop and really think about the culture we are building in our own classrooms? We will spend time on our scope and sequence, our assessment calendars, and our weekly lesson plans. But are we really intentional about the culture we are building inside the walls of our school?

In the years since I began working with schools in my current capacity as a coach, consultant, and speaker, I have really dug into what makes a difference in the culture of our schools. I think I can break it down to these two things: 1) you have got to be clear about what it is you are looking for, what you expect, and what you are trying to accomplish; and 2) you have to be very intentional with how you pursue those things. We cannot leave culture to chance anymore. We must take specific actions *on purpose* to affect the changes we want to see in our classrooms and in our schools. In the coming chapters, we will get very clear about what we believe to be important in our schools and give you very specific steps you can take to make that difference a reality.

Katie and I talked with educators from all over, and asked them to share their insights. Twenty-three of them were brave enough to write from their hearts, and put their names to something truly amazing. These are the keys to unlocking a culture-first classroom. In this book, we are sharing with you not only the how and the why but the heart of building a classroom focused on learning, leadership, safety, and ownership. We are showing you how to build a culture first classroom. So, let's go!

#roadtoawesome

Darrin and I stand on stages all over the country. We are grateful to get to do this work and be in community with educators. Leadership workshops, keynote speeches, baby (new) teacher trainings, conferences, convocations, monthly coaching, and much more has led us to know one very important fact: your best PD is the teacher down the hall. Full Stop! We have a lot of noise thrown at us as educators, negative noise that can eat away at our hearts, our souls, and frankly, our will to do this life-saving work with kids every day. Some people who think they know what it is like to walk a mile in our teacher shoes because they once sat in a classroom thirty years prior, can hurl vitriol at us. Sometimes, we can't help, but get pulled into sadness or negativity, but we can do something that Darrin and I implore you to do every day. Relentlessly celebrate and promote the positives on your campuses. Brag on your kids, go see the teacher of the year, put your teacher besties on blast for doing amazing things in their classrooms. Find the professional learning that uplifts while giving you practical tools to implement in your classrooms the very next day. Because friends, that is happening all over our nation - teachers, principals, superintendents making a big difference in their corner of the world, doing what is right for children. With this book, we bring you some of the most innovative educators we know with insights on culture, management, practical implementation, and hope. Because hope is a thing with feathers that perches in the soul and sings a tune without words and never stops. You are our children's hope and best avenue for their eventual success. So, teach on, beautiful warriors; we are rooting for you. Enjoy!

#thattealglasseslady
#untoldteachingtruths

STEP IN AND JOIN THE RANKS
Tim Collier
Academic Design Coordinator

"Constant effort and frequent mistakes are the stepping stones to genius." ~Elbert Hubbard

"You've got to get your butt behind you." This advice from my father turned out to mean that I should lift with my glutes and thighs instead of my back when handling heavy, fragile building materials. That was just one nugget of wisdom bestowed upon me by a skilled craftsman while I worked as a tradesman to pay my way through college. Those hints were always offered just when I needed them to move my skill in the trade to the next level.

If you have picked up this book, you must be ready to take the next step in your teaching and leading career. In these pages, walk with Katie Kinder and Darrin Peppard as they show you research-tested pedagogies as well as show you the color, joy, and heartbreak of this beautiful work. Not from an academic standpoint but from the perspective of seasoned, highly-skilled practitioners, you stand to learn how to embrace the sticky, broken, funny, engaging, and ultimately fulfilling calling that is upon you.

Worried that you could never be like Katie and Darrin? Well, that reminds me of another story.

"Can you not catch her, Son?" were the only words my seventy-year-old uncle could remember his dad saying as he related the story of when he, as a young teen, failed again to catch his mare. Uncle Vernon continued to spin his yarn: "I was so mad I was shaking when Dad took the rope from my hand, walked the length of the barn, hooked the lead onto the horse's halter, and led her to me. I thought Dad must have been gifted with some special magic, but it turned out that, having seen that I was ready to learn, Dad taught me one step at a time the magic of how to handle myself and my animal so she and I could both have a good day at work."

If you are ready to learn the magic of how to handle yourself and your students to build a genuinely impactful classroom and school, Katie and Darrin along with many others will show you the way. Through these pages, walk with these educators into the engaging family they create in classrooms and schools all over the nation. Study these chapters to continue on your journey to join Katie Kinder and Darrin Peppard among the ranks of master teachers.

CHAPTER ONE

More than Just
Classroom Management

At the time I wrote this, I was teaching a course at the collegiate level called Advanced Classroom Management. It's a master's level course taken by students who are earning their master's degrees as non-traditional education majors. When I was first asked to teach the course, I began reflecting on what I felt I knew about classroom management, what I had discovered over the years as a teacher, building level leader, and even as a district leader. I could see in my own mind being handed the keys to room 205 at Kingman Junior High back in 1995, walking through the door for the first time, so ecstatic to have my very own classroom. I was reminded of a variety of interactions that first year and how I felt so totally unprepared to lead in my room. I was really hung up on what I was supposed to teach, eighth grade science and math, and not sure where to begin. When we graduate with our degree or certification in teaching, we should be ready to lead a classroom, right?

It is quite possible that classroom management has gotten a bad reputation. I asked my college students what they thought of when they heard that term. Their answers didn't really surprise me all that much. I read things like how to respond to bad behavior, keeping students in line and in control, and other similar responses. Don't get me wrong, they aren't incorrect, per se, it's that we have created this thought thread about control and management of a classroom where teachers must be The Boss in the room to ensure students comply with their rules. Now, do I think all teachers approach classroom management in this way? No. I do think the best teachers view leading their classroom, building culture in their classroom, and focusing on community as a key to teaching and learning.

If you are a teacher who is new to the profession, you most likely remember your first day in front of your students quite vividly. Those of us who've been around for a while probably have a bit of a rose-colored remembrance of that day. However, the odds are strong that it went pretty similar for all of us. We learn so much in college and yet find when it is time to actually greet kids in our room that we can feel overwhelmed and unsure of ourselves. It is our contention that any teacher, veteran or baby teacher, should begin with a focus on the culture of the classroom and work from that point forward. To define the term, classroom culture is the collective values found in the room, the procedures, processes, expectations, and so forth that create the daily vibe in the room. The culture of the classroom begins with the teacher, setting clear expectations, intentionally teaching how they want students to treat each other, to communicate, and to keep each other safe. But culture is much more than just procedures and expectations. Culture is about community, collaboration, collective efficacy and accountability, even how we celebrate is a key part of the culture in our classroom.

In most cases, teachers develop the culture in the classroom as a part of ongoing work through the course of the year. This book is designed to be something different. It's built to challenge the laissez-faire approach to culture, using clarity and intentionality to get the results teachers are looking for. You can control the culture in your room, especially if you do it on purpose. The contributors to this book, along with both Katie and me, are here to guide, encourage, and push you to build the very best classroom culture possible, by putting culture first. We will provide some insight and inspiration for our newest teachers along with some fun reminders, igniters, and more for all levels of classroom teaching experience. Welcome to your Culture First Classroom.

Reflection Questions:

1. What is your first memory of leading a classroom? Were you a substitute teacher? Student teacher? What has changed for you since that time?
2. What do you think of when you hear the phrase classroom management? Has that view shifted over the course of your career?
3. What is one thing you are most hoping to find in this book?

Chapter One Notes:

_____
_____
_____
_____
_____
_____
_____

CHAPTER TWO

A Tale of Two Superintendents

I met with two superintendents on the same day to discuss professional development for their districts. My experience with each of them was vastly different, to say the least.

I walked up to one district office to have my meeting with Superintendent One. I was buzzed in the front door and spoke with the first gatekeeper.

"Hi," I said cheerfully, "I'm here to see Mr. S."

"Do you have an appointment?"

"I actually do."

"Wait here," was the reply. I sat in the first waiting room staring at plaques on the walls and leafing through an old magazine when the second gatekeeper rounded the corner.

"Come with me, Ms. Kinder," she said. "Mr. S will see you soon." I followed her click-clacketing down the hall and walked into the superintendent's waiting area. I almost gasped at how beautifully decorated it was. A velvet green, overstuffed couch sat against one wall. Sconces were draped on either side of the gatekeeper's desk. Low lighting cascaded down from the ceiling and beautiful light fixtures you would see in a fancy home graced the ceilings; not the fluorescent lights in his district's classrooms. Classical music wafted through the speakers.

"Would you like a bottle of water while you wait?" Gatekeeper Two said to me.

"Yes," I responded, "that would be nice." She leaned back, opened a stainless steel refrigerator, and grabbed me a drink.

"Thanks," I said. As I unscrewed the lid to my mini Pellegrino, Gatekeeper Number THREE appeared out of nowhere.

"You can follow me," she said, "Mr. S can see you now." I walked through a dimly lit hall, through two more doors when she opened a heavy oak door. There he sat in his three piece suit behind a beautiful mahogany executive desk. As I situated myself in a small chair in front of him, I thought to myself that his desk probably cost more than all the furniture in my whole classroom. Desks I was duct taping back together on a regular basis when I got, yet another new student, in my largest class of 36 kids smashed into a classroom built for no more than 25 students. I tried not to bristle; this was not my superintendent, but it still felt like a blow to my teacher's heart.

Do the teachers know this man? I thought to myself. *Do the kids know this man? Do the parents know this man? Does this man ever get into classrooms in his district? Does the community know this man?* Judging from his extremely expensive looking suit, the answers to my questions were, *Probably not.* I asked anyway.

"Hi, Mr. S," I said politely, "thank you for taking this meeting with me today. I've got a question for you. How often do you get into classrooms in your district? How often do you cover a class in your district? What kinds of PD do you believe your teachers need?"

He visibly scoffed. "I can't possibly sub for classes or go to classrooms for visits. I'm too busy. I'm the figurehead for this district; I don't have the time to perform such tasks." I was floored. He actually said, in words, that he was too important to trifle with such pettiness. His teachers, his kids, the parents, the community, all building blocks that make for an amazing and transformational educational experience for children, everything I'm sure he preached at each convocation seemed to be lost on this man. Mr. S had said it himself.

"Do you know the president of Devon?" He spoke sharply. Speaking about the CEO of one of the largest companies in our urban area.

"No," I stared at him bewildered, "I know Marco in third period, and I know the trauma he's been through. I know if he gets triggered, he will flip a desk or eight. I know he has goodness inside of him, and his only way out of the poverty and trauma he's found himself in *IS* his education. That is who I know, Mr. S, and another hundred kids just like him."

Mr. S gazed at me, glossed over my words, and said, "Well, I have another meeting with the president of Devon very soon." He glanced at his watch. I got the hint.

I left feeling some sadness, anger, and something else I couldn't quite put my finger on. Was it hopelessness? I thought to myself that all superintendents surely can't be like this. Some of them have to be servant leaders, people who were rock star teachers, principals, assistant superintendents. They couldn't have possibly climbed this ladder of education without loving their communities, schools, kids.

I drove thirty miles away to another district. Contemplating in my head and heart about what had just transpired with Mr. S. I pulled up to the office of the second district. I took a breath and jumped out of my car. There was only one gatekeeper at this district although just as large as the last district.

"Oh, hi, Katie Kinder," she said. "Mr. R told me you would be coming through! Unfortunately, he isn't in the office today. We were short subs, and there is a particular third grade class that gets a little unruly when their teacher isn't present, so he is covering for the day." My jaw hit the floor. She saw my shock and delight.

"Oh, he does that all the time. How can he know what professional development his teachers need if he isn't in the trenches with them?"

"You have no idea how happy this makes my heart," I whispered, "Do I need to reschedule our meeting?"

"Actually, if you are okay with it, he said you could go over to the elementary school where he is covering, and the two of you could chat while he subs."

"Absolutely!" I got back in my car and drove to one of eight elementary schools in his district. I checked in at the front office, and they escorted me to where Mr. R was teaching. He silently waved me in to have a seat with the children because Mr. R was reading *Charlotte's Web* to the students who were sitting enthralled with the cadence of his voice. He got the kids working on their collaborative group assignment after he told a few dad jokes to third graders who found themselves in stitches over his lame humor. I couldn't help myself, so I laughed too.

He ushered me over to the quintessential elementary school, half-moon table where he sat in the middle, and I grabbed a small chair and bellied up to the made-for-kids table too. He was the antithesis of Mr. S from district one. He wore rumpled khakis because he was sitting on the floor with children, a short-sleeved, pink, collared shirt, and some vintage Air Jordans. I loved him immediately.

Mr. R could tell me exactly what his teachers wanted for professional learning. Not only did he know because he was in classes and schools every day, but he knew because he sent out a survey and teachers clicked through and voted for what they wanted for their next PD day. He pulled up the chart on his iPad.

"Ninety percent of my teachers want engagement strategies and collaboration among teams, but in a fun way; that is why I called you." He smiled at me. We picked a date, shook hands, and he told the kids to wave goodbye to me.

With the kids' questions still in my ears, I smiled as I backed out of the parking lot. "Mr. R, we don't understand section two. Can you help us?" In my mind's eye, I saw his eyes squint and wrinkle in the corners, while he smiled that dad smile, "Absolutely!"

Are you a figurehead or are you a leader that rolls up your sleeves and jumps in head first to serve the teachers and students in your school, in your district? Culture goes by way of the leader. Full Stop. Which type are you? You can't affect positive change from your velvet green couch or your mahogany desk. Get out and roll those sleeves up, my friends. We get this one messy, beautiful life. What will be your legacy as a leader?

Reflection Questions:
1. Discuss the difference in the two different superintendents in this chapter.
2. As a teacher, do you want your principal to cover classes sometimes?
3. As a teacher, do you want your superintendent to cover classes?
4. Principals, if you were out for the day, would you want your superintendent to be the acting principal for the day?

5. Katie poses the question: Are you a figurehead or are you a leader that rolls up your sleeves and jumps in head first to serve students and teachers? Discuss this in your groups.
6. All adults in a school setting should be responsible for creating culture. Do you agree with this statement or not?

Chapter Two Notes:

CHAPTER THREE

Leadership that Shapes Culture

Any discussion about culture begins, in my mind, with leadership. I have stood in front of countless educators over the past handful of years and said, "If you want to change the culture in your classroom, school, lunch line, bus, or whatever your work station might be, then consider changing the way you lead it." Yes, leadership is that important in the development and sustainment of culture.

In *Culturize*, Jimmy Casas makes a strong point about ineffective leadership being the root cause of many educational issues. He also drives home the point that leadership is everyone, not just building administrators. I concur with this position and believe that everyone in the schoolhouse, regardless their title or job description, is and should be a leader. If this is true, then the reality is that everyone on campus is responsible for building and maintaining a positive culture in the school. School district leaders, superintendents and other district-office level individuals, do have a role in creating the conditions for positive culture through their communication, their presence, and what it is they look for and reinforce when they are on campus. Building administrators should be building and maintaining campus culture through their expectations, their focus on teaching and learning, how they recognize/reinforce/reward the great things happening on their campus, and through their presence. Many of the school leaders I work with are very intentional with being present in classrooms and at school activities, using their time to lean in and build relationships along with reinforcing expectations.

But where does that leave the classroom teacher? Teachers are the primary pivot position for school culture. They feel the presence and absorb the expectations from building and district leaders above them all while being the forward facing individuals working with students on a daily basis. It is in our classrooms that their leadership plays out in its most impactful way. When teachers are intentional with their ability to be leaders in the classroom and really focus on setting up and maintaining great classroom culture, students can and will thrive.

I've had the pleasure of seeing Scott Webb in action in his district many times. He is never too important for any task. He listens to his people, loves his people, and serves his people. During school days, he is in classrooms, lunchrooms, and hallways. During professional development days, he partakes in each and every activity with his staff. Enjoy his Brutal Honesty.

BRUTAL HONESTY
Scott Webb
Superintendent, Springer Public Schools

"Servant leadership is about letting your team shine bright without worrying about who gets credit for the accomplishment. In turn, servant teaching is about creating an atmosphere where all of your students shine bright."
~ Scott Webb

How can school superintendents improve school culture? To me the biggest part of influencing school culture is being open and visible. I try to walk through the buildings in my district every day. Some days, I get to sit with students in the lunchroom, and some days, I sit with my teachers in the staff break area. I tell my teachers that I am open to "brutal honesty" and sometimes they really give it to me. The key is to understand that brutal honesty is not personal. It is an honest assessment of what is wrong in our schools. I try to take that information and offer the teachers some type of response within a couple of days. The response may be "I can't fix this issue until summer break." Other times, it is "I understand the challenge you are facing from this issue. How can I help make things work better for you and your team?" The biggest part of the process is being willing to listen and to help when possible. In two years at my current district, we have already progressed from everyone just doing their job and going home into being a school where teachers are working together toward a common goal.

Action Steps

1. Be open to Brutal Honesty, like Scott; this fosters a healthy team.
2. Be willing to listen.
3. Work toward a common goal

Many of us have worked in school systems where we didn't feel the leadership was supportive or that our voice wasn't welcome. Early in my career, I worked under a superintendent who I could not have picked out of a lineup. He was completely absent from our schools. When I became an assistant principal, I was so surprised to see our superintendent and our assistant superintendent showing up on a regular basis to our campus, often they didn't even need anything - they were just there to be available. This is part of what led to my belief that, as a leader, everyone should feel seen, heard, valued, and trusted on my campus and in my district. When leaders ensure they are available, open to feedback, and are there to listen not just speak, those they lead will see them as someone they work with, not that they work for.

As Scott mentioned, school and district leaders must be willing to accept the brutal honesty of those they are charged with leading. Leadership is not just about knowing all the answers or telling people what to do. Truly great leaders will not only be open to hearing from those they lead but will actively seek out their input. This isn't just true for building and district leaders, however. In the classroom, teachers must also be open to hearing the brutal truth from their students and, on occasion, from their parents as well. None of us are infallible. We make mistakes. We sometimes ask things of our students that aren't realistic, and we have to be willing to create a space where kids feel safe telling us that.

Leadership is not about just making people happy. As Steve Jobs once said, "If you want to make people happy, don't be a leader, sell ice cream." This is where having and holding expectations, sometimes referred to as accountability, is crucial. Accountability in the school and in the classroom can take on many different forms. Our friend Charles Williams, who Katie and I both know from sharing stages and conference rooms, shares his perspective here on why accountability is so important.

Charles is one of my very favorite people in education. Over the past several years, Katie and I have both spent time with him at a variety of conferences and events. Charles represents to me what a calm, collected, and focused school leader looks and sounds like. We call him Velvet for his insanely smooth baritone voice, and he happens to be genuinely one of the best leaders out there as well as a good friend.

I met Charles Williams in 2021 via a screen. I was honored to be on his podcast not once but twice. Since that year, Darrin and I have become good friends with the man people call The Velvet Voice of Education. As a current principal and leader in this education sphere, I've seen him walk the walk as a servant leader to his teachers and his community. Enjoy his words because accountability is absolutely love in its purest of forms.

ACCOUNTABILITY IS LOVE
Charles Williams
Educator, Speaker, Friend and Officially known worldwide as The Velvet Voice of Education

"What we allow becomes culture. What we reinforce becomes tradition. What we celebrate becomes identity." ~Charles Williams

In school leadership, the culture of an institution, as noted by EduGuru Steven Bollar, is a manifestation of the traditions that shape our ideologies and guide our collective behaviors. These traditions are not random occurrences; rather, they are the result of deliberate practices consistently applied over time. In my tenure as a school administrator, I have observed that the strongest school cultures are those where these traditions are consciously nurtured and reinforced. This nurturing process involves not only setting clear expectations but also ensuring that all stakeholders - students, staff, parents, and community members - are aligned with these values.

This alignment is crucial because traditions serve as the framework within which a school operates. They influence everything from daily routines to the overarching spirit of the institution. For example, a tradition of celebrating academic achievements can create an environment that motivates all students to strive for excellence. Conversely, inconsistent enforcement of rules can lead to a culture of confusion and lack of respect for the institution. Thus, the intentional cultivation of positive traditions is fundamental to fostering a cohesive and supportive school culture.

Another cornerstone of the culture within the schools I lead is the principle that "accountability is love," a concept articulated by educator and advocate Hotep Benzo. This principle insists that truly caring for individuals within our community means holding them to the highest standards of conduct and achievement. It is about expecting the best from our students and staff and supporting them in reaching these expectations. Accountability, under this framework, is not punitive but supportive; it's a form of showing deep care and commitment to the development of each individual.

A recent incident with a student at my school illustrates this approach. A senior student wished to leave campus without adhering to our sign-out policy, suggesting instead that a phone call from her mother was adequate. I had to explain the importance of following established procedures, not just for compliance but for her safety and well-being. Our policies are in place to protect students, and circumventing them can have serious implications, both legally and personally. When she resisted, I stood firm, not out of rigidity but out of a responsibility to safeguard her, which is a manifestation of our love and care for our students.

Eventually, the student approached me to apologize for her earlier defiance. During our conversation, I shared that my youngest child was only two years older than her, emphasizing that my perspective is not only that of an administrator but also of a father. This personal insight seemed to help her understand that my actions were rooted in a paternal concern for her safety and well-being. Her acknowledgment of this care, and her expression of gratitude, underscored the effectiveness of blending accountability with empathy.

I share this story because it emphasizes the importance of steadfastness in our values and practices. The culture of our schools is a reflection of what we consistently do and what we stand by. It can evolve positively or deteriorate based on our actions and decisions. Therefore, it is imperative that we craft our school culture with intentionality and precision. We must balance firmness with understanding and discipline with compassion, always remembering that holding our students accountable is one of the highest forms of love we can offer.

Action Steps:

1. Celebrate academic achievement in your school/district.
2. Be steadfast in your values for teachers and students.
3. Balance firmness with kindness, and know that accountability is one of the highest forms of love.

One of the biggest fallacies of leadership is the belief that we have to make everyone happy. I have worked with teachers and school leaders who were such great people but who just couldn't hold anyone to a standard. I really believe that leadership comes down to being very clear about what matters and what is expected followed by being very intentional with actions and communication. Accountability, as described by Charles, is when both clarity and intentionality come to life.

The very best classroom cultures are not built on teachers simply making students happy. Many of the schools I work with currently have a few of those teachers who you might describe as trying to be friends with their students. This is especially true in middle and high schools. Teachers who struggle to set expectations and hold students to them are the ones administrators report need support with classroom management. This is where leadership becomes so important. As the teacher in the classroom, the primary adult, it is your job to be clear about what you are looking for (expect) and then to be intentional reinforcing when it happens (yes, reinforce the good things). Later, we will talk about relationships (Chapter 4), but any good leader knows you have to build relationships with people in order to truly lead them. If you are not investing in those relationships and developing the culture you wish to have in your room, then management is what you will get. Managers tell, managers direct. Leaders guide and create opportunity. Let me share an example.

Classroom manager: in this scenario, the teacher is a high school teacher (science) and focuses most of her time on getting students to comply with the rules. The teacher has a good lesson structure but will stop for any minor issue (addressing a quick glance at a cell phone, a student slightly off task, etc) and eventually will call the student out in front of the class to reprimand them for off-task behaviors.

Classroom leader: in this scenario, the teacher is also a high school science teacher and focuses most of his time on getting students to his desired learning goal. He moves around the room checking in with students but does not allow small issues to district him or the other students. If a student is off-task significantly, this teacher addresses it in a one-on-one conversation while other students continue to work and progress toward the learning goal.

Each teacher will have to develop their own style of leading in the classroom. But it is in the small details, the way the teacher chooses to focus on compliance or learning, that will be a driver in the culture of these two classrooms. In honesty, these are both rooms I have been in, teachers I have worked with. As a leader of the school, you knew what I was looking for and hoping would happen. I want all teachers to be classroom leaders, not classroom managers.

Again, each will lead in their own way. In this next passage, Tim Perdue shares why it is so important for every teacher, every leader, to find their own personality and allow it to come through in their leadership and their development of culture.

When I was a baby teacher back in 2006, I often hesitated to ask for help, believing that I should already have all the answers. I struggled with the fear that admitting uncertainty would reflect poorly on me. But there was one administrator I could always turn to - Tim Perdue. Tim treated his teachers with genuine care and compassion, and I knew I could approach him with any question, trusting he would respond with kindness and understanding. He truly led by example, and it's an honor to share his thoughts on leadership and learning with you today.

BE A MODEL FROM THE TOP
Tim Perdue
Educator, Principal, Author

*"If we want our children to move mountains
we first
have to let them get out of their chairs."
~Nicolette Sowder*

*"Your visions will become clear only when you
can look into your own heart. Who looks
outside, dreams;
who looks inside, awakes."
~C.G. Jung*

I will never forget how accomplished I felt after graduating college and passing my teacher certification test. I remember saying, "I'm ready to change the world!" Little did I know what the next 34 years held for me as an educator. I had the best preparation anyone could have. My mom was an elementary school principal, and I had an incredible student teaching experience. To top it off, I had a lot of experience with teachers and principals due to my mischievous behavior as a kid. I found out quickly that there was much more to becoming a successful teacher and educator than just showing up.

During my student teaching experience, I was fortunate to serve under three different teachers. Most of the time, student teachers had one mentor teacher to learn from, but I was blessed to have three. I still remember some lessons I learned as a student teacher: I need to know my curriculum and have classroom management skills. Fortunately, I loved teaching social studies and knew how to develop good relationships with students. The relationship piece came naturally with the sense of humor that I developed growing up.

Since I did not want to coach, finding a social studies position would be difficult. It wasn't long before I landed my first job as a middle school social studies teacher. I was excited, thankful, and blessed to find a position teaching the curriculum I loved. The principal didn't take long after the school year started to ask me about coaching football. I accepted the offer. I only wanted to teach but knew I needed to help the school. At that point, I started learning by teaching more than the subjects I loved. I was about to ride on the roller coaster that would eventually mold me into an educator.

One of the first lessons I learned happened during my coaching career. For the first four years of teaching and coaching, I was privileged to be the assistant to someone I felt was very successful in the coaching realm. He was a successful coach with high standards and was like a drill sergeant in many ways. He hated to lose, wanted to win, and didn't want anyone or anything to stand in his way. I describe his style as the Vince Lombardi type. Work hard, and do it my way. It was unbelievable because together we made a good team. I learned about organizing, time management, and working hard. He made coaching fun. Over the course of our time together, I continued to be his loyal assistant, and during that time, our teams remained very successful.

Things had been going great in the classroom and on the football field. But after my fourth year, I learned that, like everything else in life, the faculty of the school changes, and people leave. That's what happened after my fifth year. Vince Lombardi left, and I became the head football coach and athletic director. Now, I was in charge of the football team and all the athletic programs for the school. That was not something I had ever planned to do when I started my career in education.

There was no time to waste. It was August, and it was time to start football practice and school. Luckily, I had two young assistants with similar personalities who had also been coaching at the school for the past couple of years and were going to help coach again. Before we knew it, it was time to have parent meetings and begin the season. We were excited and ready to start the new challenge, but the only frame of reference we had to learn from was our former supervising coach and his coaching style. We tried to be three hard-nosed coaches using the same coaching style as the person we had learned from. It couldn't have been more disastrous, and everything backfired. We were out there not having fun while trying to be like someone we weren't. The team's morale was not good, and it was evident in every aspect of the program. Things had to change. I will never forget our meeting and discussing why things weren't going as planned. I remember talking with the other coaches and saying, "You know I am so different from our previous coach. I'm not a hard-nosed type of person or educator. I believe in cutting up and having fun. I'm not as structured as our faux Vince Lombardi." What great discussions we had during that meeting. It was like we were confessing our sins. Our reflection during that meeting was probably the start of the foundation I built as an educator. Talk about collaboration.

Although we greatly respected our previous head coach and knew he had a huge heart for kids, we couldn't coach like he did. We had to use our talents and skills and be ourselves. Our meeting was very successful. It was a model for collaboration. We developed a plan for the next day, which included some of the most nontraditional football drills in the sport's history. The following practice was one of the most fun I remember in my long career. We cheered, laughed, motivated kids, used adolescent psychology, and had fun. Wind sprints became passing and receiving drills with all players. Running wasn't looked at as punishment or hard work anymore. We made it fun, and the kids didn't even know it was happening. But guess what? They were getting in shape. Have you ever seen a 250-pound lineman catch a pass? They loved it!

The entire team was running, getting in shape, and having the time of their lives. Making things fun, motivating, and cheering players along the way increased morale instantly. I will never forget that after the practice that day, every player went into the locker room thinking they would be the next NFL superstar. The high five the other coaches and I gave each other that day will remain in our memory forever. Each of us learned a great lesson. The difference between that day and the ones in the past is that we made our players feel good about themselves and have an abundance of confidence. It didn't mean that there would not be challenges along the way, but developing a positive culture in whatever you do will help everyone get through the hard days. We continued incorporating new ideas and drills as the season went on. We actually won football games, and when it was all said and done, we were competitive and successful. It was so much fun!

So, what did we learn? We learned that as an educator, you have to be yourself. Students and players know when you are not authentic and trying to be someone else. It's only natural that things will go smoother when you are authentic and utilizing your own gifts. Planning is essential. Develop ideas for the strategies you want to incorporate while reaching your goals.

When I took the time to reflect on the changes we made with our coaching philosophy, I thought, why not carry it over to the classroom? That is what I did. We learned, had fun, and incorporated numerous activities while reaching our goals. You will be successful when you are authentic, enthusiastic, encouraging, willing to try anything to help students, and most of all, having fun. I collaborated with other teachers on best practices in the classroom. Collaboration with a common goal is a crucial factor in being successful. Reflecting on areas of success and those areas for improvement are resolved better when you have others to work with.

Another valuable lesson occurred when I became the director of a campus at a technology center. Most of our students were high school students, but we also had a percentage of adult students who attended programs alongside those still in high school. At the start of the new role, one of my goals was to change students' perception of administrators. Several times, I had negative experiences with students due to their previous interactions with former administrators. When I mentioned the concern to my assistant, I recognized that she had the same problem regarding student perceptions of administrators. There were also expectations from some instructors that the only way to discipline a student was to suspend or remove them from school. It was very challenging to deal with both of these perceptions. As an administrator, I felt trapped between trying to develop relationships with students and supporting teachers. I will never forget the feeling I had the first few weeks of school while walking down the hall. Students look at you as if you are a big, bad boss who is out to get them. I hope you have never experienced this feeling because it does not relate to or help develop a positive culture. There needs to be mutual trust between students and teachers. So, what did we do? We had to promote a positive climate intentionally. My assistant and I had to get out of our office and start moving, as well as model a positive attitude and safe environment. I made it a priority to visit every class during the morning and afternoon. I made it a point to speak to and smile at every student and visit with the teacher. I will admit to not being the most organized person or the best at time management, but I decided to put off the paperwork and build a positive school climate as my primary goals.

Getting into the hallways to visit students and teachers daily takes work and self-discipline. I prioritized visiting classrooms and teachers each day regardless of the paperwork I had waiting for me in the office. It didn't always make the upper administration happy, but it was best for my campus. It wasn't long before students recognized me as someone who truly cared for them. I remember seeing a difference within the first six weeks of school. One thing I recognized with this initiative is that when you genuinely get to know students and teachers and work to develop relationships, it makes a difference in what happens during the school day. I lost the feeling of being the disciplinarian. I got to know the students and learned how to support them.

The trust between students, staff, and administrators blossomed. When this happens, nothing is impossible. It is a feeling that makes you want to get up early and go to work. It was indeed a cohesive, positive atmosphere. I am not saying there were never issues, but it was easier to get through the issues when the framework was already developed for an environment based on respect and appreciation.

Another thing I learned is that the leader sets the tone of the campus, not just with the faculty but with the students and parents. Staying focused on making students, teachers, parents, and visitors feel welcomed and appreciated will go a long way toward providing a remarkable school climate. We were having our annual back-to-school celebration, and I remember a large group of students playing ping pong.

They were loud, rowdy, and having fun. There was one particular student who was providing a play-by-play in Spanish. It was glorious! He was animated and enthusiastic and having the time of his life. The students who gathered around the table were laughing and smiling. I remember walking through the area, and one student yelled, "Hey, Mr. Perdue wants to play!" I immediately approached the table and said, "Let's go!" The students who were having such fun might make a traditional educator nervous. They were screaming, yelling, and chanting with excitement, all in Spanish, but I loved it. From that day forward, I knew we had made a difference and were making steps in the right direction. It wasn't about who was breaking the rules and who needed a behavior referral to the office. It was about making every day and every moment count with students.

When the school's attitude changes, so does the morale, behavior, attendance, and progress. I knew that maintaining a positive attitude and connecting with everyone would have a lasting effect. Everyone plays a role in developing the school's positive culture, but it has to be a model from the top. Students, teachers, and parents must see it in action every day. Yes, we all make mistakes and must learn from them, but how you rebound from them makes a difference. When you develop a positive culture within a school, it benefits everyone. The climate turns from punitive and negative to one focused on being kind and respectful toward each other. It is natural that when you focus on the positive, students will feel more comfortable and secure, which will positively impact learning. Another thing I learned about developing and maintaining a positive school environment is that you must not worry about your pride, and be willing to forgive others as well as yourself. It reminds me of one of my favorite quotes by Brené Brown, "Forgiveness is not forgetting or walking away from accountability or condoning a hurtful act; it's the process of taking back and healing our lives so we can truly live."

Action Steps:

1. Lean into who you are; don't try to be someone else. It won't work.
2. Be visible, like Tim Perdue.
3. Forgive early and often.

During my tenure as a building principal, I had a small portion of my staff that wasn't always in my corner. There are all kinds of theories behind this type of human behavior, where no matter what you don't get everyone on board with your direction. There were, in my case, five members of the staff that seemed to oppose nearly everything I would bring forward in efforts to improve our school's performance. I worked hard to lean into them, believing that most of those we label as obstinate or not on board simply need to feel heard. Ultimately, that led to my focus on ensuring everyone on campus felt seen, heard, valued, and trusted.

One particular year, when preparing to hire an assistant principal, I placed one of my five most outspoken critics on the hiring team on purpose. I had asked each member to review all the files of each candidate we were planning to interview. The hope was that they'd feel ownership of the hire and would have some insights when they came to the table for the interview. When my critic came to my office to review files, I had scheduled some time to catch up on emails and a budget report, so I stayed while she read the files. After about 30 minutes she asked me a question about which of the 30 or so candidates I felt best fit our school. I told her I didn't want to shape the committee's thinking and declined to answer. She said, "Darrin, I trust you and know you will always do what is best for our staff, students, and school."

WOW, that sent a shock wave through my body!

I learned that in her case, and in each of the other cranky crew members, they supported me yet maybe needed more TLC, more opportunity for their voice to be heard. I doubled down on going to them any time I was considering a change. That doesn't mean they always got their way, frequently they didn't. But I learned a huge lesson in the power of trust and how we build it with our adults on campus. The reality is, it works with kids too. Listening, creating opportunities to be heard, and encouraging meaningful input makes a tremendous difference in relationships and the culture of a campus.

Leadership is critical in the development of culture on our campuses. As Tim shared in his passage, we have to figure out who each of us is and how we wish to lead. Every teacher, coach, principal, and superintendent goes through the process of getting comfortable with who they are and how they will live up to their own expectations. It can be a monumental struggle figuring out who we want to be in the classroom. But the steps shared in this chapter can take us a long way toward figuring out who we are and how we wish to lead our culture first classroom.

Reflection Questions:

1. Do you think of yourself as a leader from your position?
2. In what ways are you leading with an open perspective?
3. How can you ensure that your expectations of yourself and others are clear and that you help everyone reach those expectations?
4. Do you feel like you have reached a point where you are clear about who you are and how you want to lead?
5. In what ways are you ensuring a culture of trust is being developed in your school and in your classroom?

Chapter Three Notes:

CHAPTER FOUR

Relationships as the
Heart of Culture

Early in my career as a building principal, I had a team of assistant principals who oversaw much of our day-to-day operations. Student discipline was one of those responsibilities I had delegated to my team. While we had done a considerable amount of work to strengthen the culture and climate in our school, we still had student discipline issues that rose to the level of administrative intervention. Frequently, my APs would ask teachers what they had done to build a relationship with a student prior to sending them to the office. *Okay, okay. I know this might cause many teachers to throw the BS flag.* Many of you have probably heard that from a building level leader too. What you should know is, as a building leader, I never felt that not building a teacher-student relationship was an adequate reason not to address the student behavior at the administrative level. Rather, I think it is important to know how much of a student's story the teacher is aware of, as well as the level of knowledge the administrator has of the student's background. Frequently, the building administrator may know more about a student than the teacher does. However, it may well go in the opposite direction. My philosophy here is that teachers and administrators must work together to know as much as possible in order to surround the student with support rather than use relationships as a word to volley back and forth and compare who might have more information. It is not a competition, nor is this a time when we should be shunting any responsibilities (on either side of the desk) as they pertain to one of our students. In short, administrators: don't shirk your responsibilities and push office referrals back telling a teacher to build a relationship first; teachers: don't assume you know more about the student than the administrator does. Share your knowledge, and work together on behalf of kids.

As educators we know relationships are the heart of real learning, of culture, of everything we do as we serve the people entrusted to us, but sometimes, in real-life situations and in real-time practice, relationships can be hard to build and maintain. The connections forged between students, teachers, and peers shape not only the academic experience but also personal growth, emotional well-being, and lifelong learning habits. A classroom where relationships are nurtured becomes a dynamic space where students feel safe, motivated, and engaged in their education. It is with this mindset that we brought the educators, teachers, and principals to you that have been able to catch lightning in a bottle when it comes to relationships.

Strong teacher-student relationships contribute to higher academic performance. Teachers who invest time in understanding their students' strengths and weaknesses can tailor instruction to meet individual needs, ultimately leading to improved academic outcomes, but more importantly improved health, wellness, and joy in the people around us.

Unlike most of these amazing contributors, I have actually worked in the same building with Tonya. She and I worked together for a number of years at Rock Springs High School. Tonya was not only a great advocate for kids and a super special education teacher, she became a trusted friend and colleague. As a building leader, it is important that you have your people. The ones you can go to for insight, to vent to, and lean on for an occasional reality check. Tonya was one of those people for me. Additionally, she played a big part in reshaping the culture of our school. I'm honored to know Tonya and consider her a great friend in education.

REAL-LIFE CONNECTIONS
Tonya Follum
Educator of Special Education in Wyoming

"Believe you can, and you're halfway there"
~Theodore Roosevelt

Imagine being a freshman in high school and walking into class knowing the next four years are going to be a repeat of frustration, anxiety, and failure. After 21 years as a high school special education teacher, many students enter my room thinking these very thoughts. I felt compelled to create a positive classroom culture built on strong relationships and connections to break this cycle of what I lovingly called "stinkin' thinkin'." At the heart of this endeavor was the belief in the potential of every student. Therefore, as an educator I strived to understand and embrace the unique abilities of each learner, ensuring they felt valued and respected. This belief in students' capabilities boosted their self-esteem and encouraged them to strive for success. Building strong relationships also involved consistent, open communication with students and parents. I made an effort to understand my students' interests, strengths, and challenges through one-on-one conversations, regular check-ins, and truly listening to them, not just hearing them. Equally important was the interaction and communication with parents. Similar to students, I feel parents deserve the opportunity to share their story and express their desires for their students in a safe and supportive environment. This collaboration led to a more comprehensive understanding of the students' needs and the development of strategies that extended beyond the classroom. Engaging parents as partners in the educational process cultivated a supportive network for my students. The connections made with students were deepened by integrating real-life experiences into the classroom. For instance, lessons that answered the decades-old question "When am I ever going to use this?" helped students understand the importance and practicality of what they were learning. Providing context that students could relate to and allowing for personal creativity, not only built essential life skills but made education more meaningful and fun. Inevitably, students would become frustrated with the educational process. I would explain to them that education is structured around a one-size-fits-all (straight line) approach, and they learn in a more creative (zig-zag) manner. However, creativity is not measured on standardized testing, and yet, for students in special education, creativity is generally an area of strength. In my classroom, the focus was not on standardized scores. Instead, I focused on helping my students set realistic and achievable goals geared toward their future plans. Of course, we celebrated all successes, no matter how small. Ultimately, a positive classroom culture is built on a foundation of trust, respect, and belief in each student's potential. By focusing on relationships, real-life connections, and making education enjoyable, I created an environment where students felt empowered and excited to learn. This approach not only enhanced academic performance but also nurtured personal growth. It also instilled resilience, self-belief, and the drive to achieve individual goals, while laying a foundation for lifelong success.

Action Steps:

1. Connect curriculum to the real world.
2. Have students create life goals in your classroom.
3. What lessons in your class focus on students' creativity?

Allowing our students to think critically, and express themselves creatively, like Tonya endorses, begins to open their eyes, minds, and hearts to true learning. Learning about people, walking a mile in someone else's shoes, bringing classroom cultures together by celebrating differences, and knowing our mistakes and failures bring us to eventual success leads to a school culture that is safe, full of belonging, and a place where trust fosters more trust. A classroom where proximity breeds empathy is a place that children can thrive. The relationships formed in the classroom have a lasting impact beyond the school years. A student who experiences positive relationships in school is more likely to develop healthy interpersonal skills, excel in future academic or professional settings, and build meaningful relationships throughout life. Teachers who invest in their students not only influence academic success but also shape the character and confidence of the next generation. The ripples of joy and learning continue to ebb and flow throughout the lives of children forever, and that is something we should never take lightly.

I've been blessed to work with so many amazing educators and schools over the past few years. Papillion-La Vista High School in Nebraska is one of my favorites. Principal, Jason Ryan, has a very strong team, a clear vision, and models what trust in our teachers should look and feel like. One of the strongest members of this school is Lori Boudreau. Having worked with PLVHS for over three years, I have been in her room many times. I am always struck by her ability to connect with students, lead a classroom with very high expectations, and have an environment built on trust. Plus, I always feel energized when I get to talk with Lori and watch her teach!

BUILDING TRUST IN THE CLASSROOM
Lori Boudreau
High School English Teacher, Omaha, NE

*"Education is not the filling of a pail
but the lighting of a fire."*
~William Butler Yeats

Building connections and nurturing relationships within a high school classroom are necessary for creating a positive and supportive learning environment. These connections not only enhance academic performance but also contribute to the emotional well-being and personal growth of students. The following strategies have allowed me to implement and preserve relationships in a welcoming, safe, and trusting classroom environment.

Welcoming Atmosphere

I find that when students feel welcomed, they feel more comfortable; thus, they are more apt to be engaged in the learning that is happening in the classroom. Creating a welcoming environment can be done in several ways such as greeting students at the door or after they enter the classroom. My goal is to be in the hallway during passing periods. If I'm able to do this, I say hello to *all* students as they pass by, and if I know their name, I include that in my greeting. For the students who are entering my room, I greet them and also try to ask how they are doing, tell them good luck in their game or activity that is later that day, or even compliment them on their outfit or new hair style. Many students are engrossed in their phone as they enter, but I have found that if I am consistent with my greeting, the students are prepared for it and begin to greet me first or at the very least respond to my greeting.

Classroom Layout

Teachers can be deliberate in the set up of their classroom to create strong relationships with students. As I consider my classroom layout, I want it to be student-centered and accessible for all students as well as myself. I like the idea of students being able to collaborate easily during class as well as work independently when it is needed. I am fortunate to have two large tables in my classroom for students to use while completing group work. As some students work at the tables, other students can arrange their desks in clusters. Mobility in a classroom is important so the teacher can access all students while fostering relationships. I know this can be difficult with a smaller classroom, so it's helpful to experiment with different arrangements throughout the school year. Sometimes, changes in arrangement are needed to give the room some variety, and other times, changes are needed to make sure the layout accommodates the needs of all students. For example, in my co-taught English classes, I have arranged the seating to make more room for myself and my co-teacher to work one-on-one with particular students. That might mean leaving some desks empty so the teachers can use those when assisting students during direct instruction and/or work time.

Empowering Students

Having a designated area to showcase student work helps build a sense of pride in the classroom, which in turn helps make connections. In my classroom, I have three bulletin boards on the back wall that serve this purpose. Displaying student work is a great way to get students talking about what they're learning in class, to demonstrate for visitors (parents, administrators, other teachers) what learning is taking place, and of course, to simply provide some decoration for the room. Showing student work fosters confidence in students and can be empowering. Another way to encourage students is to provide them with opportunities to lead class activities and discussions. This can be empowering because it allows students to demonstrate their skills and strengths while allowing them to have choices in their learning.

Getting to Know Students and Building Trust

It can be a daunting task each year to really get to know each of your students; however, it is one of the most integral parts to building successful relationships and ultimately enhancing student learning. There are several things I focus on in order to know my students and build trust in the classroom. Learning the names of my students along with the correct pronunciations is one of my first priorities at the beginning of the school year. Within the first three days, it is my goal to master this. The easiest way for me has been to place students in an alphabetized seating chart. While they are doing some group and independent get-to-know-you activities, I am studying names and faces. After three days, I leave the room while the students sit at different desks; when I re-enter, I say all of their names. With each passing year, this becomes a little more difficult for me, but it's really fun for the kids and helps create the foundation for our relationship building. Another way I get to know my students is with interest surveys at the beginning of the year. These surveys give me an idea of students' interests, likes, strengths, and goals. I use this information to connect to students and support them throughout their time in my class. Along with interest surveys, I try to do impromptu personal check-ins throughout the year; this is a way for me to gauge how students are doing on a regular basis. With these quick conversations throughout the year, trust is consistently built and the teaching and learning process is enhanced. One other opportunity for building trust in my classroom is the ability for students to work in groups to complete tasks. Group projects require students to communicate and collaborate with each other, many times interacting with others who might be out of their comfort zone.

Summary

As teachers, you are implementing many of these strategies and many more every day without even thinking about it. It's always a good idea to take some time to pause and consider the teaching strategies you use each day and why you use them. The approaches mentioned above can build trust within your classroom and encourage positive relationships with your students. In turn, this can improve student engagement, motivation, and general success in the classroom.

Action Steps:
1. Greet students at the door every day.
2. Be intentional about your classroom layout.
3. Teach students how to lead classroom activities to foster trust.

Are we considering what our actual space looks like? Lori intentionally set up a space that fosters learning. Darrin has seen it in action, and Lori goes on to explain that trust is a cornerstone in the success of her students. Trust is the bedrock of a successful classroom. When students and teachers establish trust, the learning environment transforms into a safe, supportive, and engaging space where students feel empowered to explore, express themselves, and take academic risks. Trust enhances communication, builds confidence, and strengthens relationships, making it a fundamental component of effective education. Trust is the great multiplier; any dynamic and successful team thrives when a great sense of trust is in place. It should be no different for our children in a classroom. It is also important to remember that just because we have established high amounts of trust, doesn't mean things will always go smoothly. This is messy, human work, and conflict is inevitable, but how we deal with that conflict makes all the difference in our schools; how we teach our children to deal with that conflict makes all the difference in their lives.

As I think about relationships and their impact on culture building, I am drawn back to my time as a classroom teacher. I was a middle school science teacher for five years, followed by teaching high school science for six more years. I transitioned between the two roles in the same community, so for a period of time, I had a group of students for upwards of six years. Many of my students either were in my class or were on some of the athletic teams I coached during that time. When you can build that kind of consistency it is amazing what happens with the relationships.

My daughter was born, our amazing Liz, the day before I interviewed for my position at the high school. So, it was during that first year teaching high school biology that I had *one of those days*. Any of us who are parents know there were times early in our kids' lives that they did not sleep well. The child might be colicky, gassy, teething, or just plain fussy. Regardless of the reason, it results in very little sleep for the child as well as the grown ups. After one of those very nights, my third period class just would not settle down and get focused. I had known most of these kids since they were in the eighth grade (now most were in 11th grade). Through my frustration and lack-of-sleep induced fog, I said something to the effect of *Guys, today isn't the day to cross me*. A football player in the class named JT, stood up and informed the class that, "Pep is having a bad day, and we are all just gonna shut up and do what Pep says, or I will wreak havoc on whoever crosses him." The class was awesome the rest of the period. While I wouldn't recommend this tactic, this was only possible and only happened because of the relationship I had built with JT and his classmates over a period of time. They knew I needed their help much more that day than they needed mine. I did eventually thank JT, although I did tell him he could have found a bit better way to address the situation.

Relationships are paramount in any journey to building classroom culture. If we, as adults, are willing to be open and a little vulnerable, our students will lean in and get to know us. The long standing phrase "kids don't care how much you know until they know how much you care" is still valid to this day. We live in a world where so many of the connections our students have are of the virtual and/or digital variety that we must do everything we can to build interest in us as human beings. As a school leader, I occasionally worked with teachers who maybe weren't as proficient as I was at building relationships with students. The truth is, I think that is what my two APs were getting at yet were unable to offer potential solutions for those who struggled. To that end, let me share these ideas, which might trigger other thoughts in your mind.

- In your classroom, share things that you care about: hobbies, favorite activities, sports teams, etc.

- Have images on the walls and around the room that invite kids to ask you questions about them: pictures of you skiing, attending a game at a particular stadium, hiking or traveling, or of your dog - everyone loves dogs.

- Add personal stories to enhance the content you are teaching in your classroom. Quick example: when I taught anatomy and physiology I shared the story of being hospitalized when I was a teacher at the junior high and how my potassium levels were so low that once replenished I had random muscle twitches for a couple of weeks. I used this story when talking about action potential in muscle tissue and since many of my students had me in junior high, they connected back to when I was out of school for two weeks.

- School leaders: this one is for you! At a school in Texas, I once saw that each teacher had a personalized door sign. I brought that idea back to my school. Every teacher, para, custodian, lunch staff, secretary, etc. had an 8 ½ x 11 inch plastic frame mounted outside their door. Their task was to create their own door sign. My only requirements were for them to have a picture of themselves, list their degrees and colleges/universities, and what they taught. However, nearly every single one had personal information, colors and logos of their colleges, pictures of their kids. What a fun way for people to learn more about your staff. Parents loved it, kids loved it, and honestly, my staff loved it.

Tricia is not only an incredible teacher but also someone whose presence brings warmth and joy to everyone around her. At Steve Woolf's Wild Heart Teacher Retreat, we had the privilege of experiencing Tricia's radiant spirit firsthand. It's truly an honor to share her wise words on teaching and her reminder to never overthink the small stuff.

NEVER OVERTHINK THE SMALL STUFF
Tricia Phelps
Teacher, Licking Valley High School

"Be vulnerable with your story to build relationships because they are the foundation to all school and classroom culture."
~Tricia Phelps

Let's be real with one another; the educational experience is not the same for all students. Yet, students are asked to attend school daily without understanding the true framework of what our professional goals might be for them besides reaching that stage for graduation. I have found that as a high school teacher, the greatest measurement of my success while being their teacher is what the students might share as a reflection of their own experience while being in my classroom. They may not share their favorite lesson that I presented to them. However, they may tell me that they still have the selfie we took together at homecoming, say thank you for sharing my snacks from my desk or the positive sticky note I gave them on Motivational Monday, or an appreciation for me taking the time to come to their choir concert. I am reminded as I read these responses each year that the little things I do matter to them. Being kind, being authentic, and simply being present is what students want to observe from the adults in their lives. I want my students to remember my passion for teaching as I share a smile with them and a high five at the door when they enter. When they leave for the day, I remind them I will look forward to seeing them again tomorrow. Let's never overthink the small stuff and never stress out about the big stuff. Just keep showing up to school each day for the kids, and in the end, graduation will happen, and we will celebrate this milestone with all of our kids together. They say it takes a village to raise a child, and I say the possibility of one teacher who has built a genuine connection or a relationship could change the mindset of one student.

Action Steps:
1. Be present today, like Tricia.
2. Don't forget that the small things become the big things.
3. Tell students you are looking forward to seeing them tomorrow.

Remembering Tricia's words is an important reminder that the small things are the big things when students look back on their education. They will remember if you smiled and seemed happy to be there; they will remember if you greeted them at the door, and worked hard on their behalf. They will also remember if you seemed to not like them or did not greet them. I often ask my audiences to reflect on their own education; some of us have to go back further than others in our memories. I always love hearing their tales about their teachers who loomed larger than life, the ones that inspired them to get into teaching. However, every once in a great while I will have a teacher whisper to me, "I became a teacher because I was treated horribly as a student and I wanted to change that for future generations; I wanted to bring about kindness and joy because it was not brought forth for me." Goodness! That hits hard. We want to be remembered for the smiles, high fives, engaging lessons, and the positive relationships that we forged not for negative ones.

I first met Jay at Steve Woolf's Wild Heart Teacher Retreat in the summer of 2021. Jay and I bonded over stories, struggles, and a lot of caramel whiskey. Since that time, Jay and I have forged a great friendship and he's become someone who I admire as an educator, as a speaker, and as a human being.

IT. STARTS. WITH. ME!
Jay B. Gross
High School Teacher, MI

Jay's former students shared this about him: "Jay Gross embodies lifelong relationships. He allows students' dreams and aspirations to lead their learning. When they leave Jay's guidance they are ready to attack the world. This is coming from a former student and lifelong friend of 30+ years." ~Jamey Nelson

After 34 years in the classroom, I know one thing for sure; it starts with me! Now, remember, as you read this you are dealing with a guy who lives WAY outside the box. I eat my KitKat bar by biting right into it, NOT breaking it off piece by piece. Many people use the tried and true ways to create classroom culture. I do what needs to be done.

I have continually tried to have my students see me as a person, not just an information deliverer. Once, when I was a student teacher, I was shopping at Meijer early on a Saturday morning. I ran into a young student and her parents in the produce section. I can still picture her face when she saw me. Excited at first and yelling, "Mr. Gross! How you doing?" Within seconds her face changed to puzzled, and she looked into my cart at my stuff.

I asked, "What's the matter, Sunshine?"

She stuttered, "You... you... you shop?" I had to laugh. The look in her parents' eyes was hilarious.

As I drove home, it made me think back to when I was in school. I never thought about my teachers as actual people. They were just teachers. I vowed then and there that I would make sure my students saw me as human.

It starts with the doorway/hallway during passing periods. I love standing there and watching the students come in and pass by. I see their clothing, their backpacks, their shoes, their sporting equipment. I use these cues to start conversations. For example, a student walked in with a new pair of Steph Curry basketball shoes. I asked, "Hey! What size are those?"

With a curious look on his face, he replied, "11s."

I said, "Dang! I need 12s or I'd steal those! Nice-looking kicks, Sir!" The student's puzzled look changed to a genuine smile, and he went to his seat.

It starts with me, right down to the clothes I wear. I have shirts and hoodies with positive sayings such as, *Humankind, Be Both* and *Your Story Continues*. I cannot count how many times I have been asked, "Where did you get that shirt?" Then, they show up wearing the same shirt or a different one with another positive message. It is the Autism Awareness shirts I wear that are noticed the most. I get questions about my shirt and what autism is. I am perpetually stunned by how many kids have no clue about autism. It is an honor, helping students understand and empathize with children who live with autism.

It starts with me and my classroom. I have couches, LazyBoy chairs, tables, desks, refrigerators, and posters everywhere; including multiple poster boards with pictures of students doing amazing things, like their senior pictures and their sporting events. The kids love it when I add one of their pictures to my boards. The best part for me is when my students graduate, have kids of their own, and their children are now in my classroom laughing at their parents and the pictures of them on my walls. One of the greatest compliments I have ever received was from a former student about seven years removed from high school. She wrote to me, "I always felt safe in your classroom. It was like a home away from home to me, and you always accepted me for who I was." There is no better evaluation I can think of than that.

It starts with what I let them know about me. My screensaver and desktop have pictures of my life. There are pictures of mountains I have climbed, glaciers I have been on, me whitewater rafting and canyoning, my family, my dogs, and all sorts of pictures that let them into my world. So many questions and discussions have come about when students have seen these and inquired about my life. And one of the keys: I am sure to ask if they have been on any adventures or trips, if they have any pets, and what their families are like.

It continues with the way I teach and what I teach. I teach life. I want everything I use to somehow relate to my students' lives and how it can help them. This starts with choosing books that my students can connect with. Yes, I teach the classics and young adult literature, but I LOVE the works of Mitch Albom. I use *Tuesdays With Morrie*, *The Five People You Meet In Heaven*, *The Next Person You Meet In Heaven*, and *For One More Day*. The feedback from the kids and the projects they come up with for these books are top notch. And the thing I appreciate most is the discussions we have, each person in our classroom respecting the others' opinions and learning it is okay to have differences.

My classroom and its culture all start with me, and I wouldn't have it any other way.

Action Steps:
1. Bring your humanness into the classroom, like Jay.
2. Connect with kids using the little things, like shoes.
3. Think about what cause you can bring into your classroom to help bring awareness.

Relationships have to be the center of what we do every day. The curriculum and content must come second to learning about and loving our students for exactly who they are when they come to us. Establishing a healthy family classroom is essential. A place where big risks can be taken because when students trust their teacher, they will listen without judgment, they are more likely to share their concerns, struggles, and successes. Teachers who establish these relationships receive invaluable feedback from students, allowing them to adjust their teaching methods to better support learning needs. Our hope for you during this chapter on relationships was to learn from the best and bottle up some of that magic lightning for yourself and your classroom.

Reflection Questions:

1. We know that relationships are important. Why do some teachers scoff at the idea of building relationships?
2. We also know having high expectations for kids is doing what is right for them, so how can positive relationships help students with trust and achievement?
3. Tell your relationship stories. Our stories matter, your students' stories matter, so share your success stories with your people.
4. Compare and contrast our contributors in this chapter: Tonya, Lori, Tricia, and Jay, and think about how you can use their approaches in your school.

Chapter Four Notes:

_____
_____
_____
_____
_____
_____
_____
_____
_____
_____

CHAPTER FIVE

Inclusive and Intentional Environments

When I was in the fourth grade, I had arguably the worst school year of my life. I was a really good student, not the best but quite good. Yet my teacher did not seem to like me. I continually received negative feedback, dripping red on my work. I tried to work harder, but it didn't improve. In fact, it got worse, at one point I was trying to fake illnesses just so I didn't have to go to school. When my mom decided she'd had enough, she went and met with my principal and my teacher. While things maybe got a little better after that, I really had lost my confidence and didn't feel welcome in my classroom. Years later, my mom shared that my fourth-grade teacher had lost her son to suicide during that time, and I somehow reminded her of him. She was directing her anger toward me, even though I really wasn't doing anything wrong.

When sixth grade rolled around, I vowed to get out of the funk and be myself again. I did well in fifth grade, and my love for school was returning. But then I met Mr. Stark, my sixth grade teacher. Not only was he the first male teacher I'd ever had, he was *so cool*! He worked very hard to make sure each and every one of us in the class felt like we belonged and were seen by him every day. I will never forget being in his classroom the day an attempt was made on President Reagan's life. With the television coverage playing in the background, he answered (or attempted to) every question inquiring sixth grade minds had about the law, government, and the impact that event might have on our country. With Mr. Stark's help, caring, and having a culture where everyone was part of something special, I got my love for school back just in time for junior high.

It is so important for students to feel like they are included and welcome in the classroom. It is that base level of safety that is the difference between students opening up, taking risks, and really growing compared to when they retreat, withdraw, and become like a ghost in our classrooms and hallways. This chapter is filled with incredible insight from amazing contributors in the field making it happen every day. As an example, Bradlee W. Skinner, who teaches high school English and theater and is a master of including all students and developing lessons that are not only engaging but that stick with students for the long haul.

I think people come into our lives for reasons that are not obvious until much later in the journey. I was blessed to hire Bradlee at Rock Springs High School and work alongside him for three years. But that is just a small part of the story. Over the years we've become friends, confidants, and have impacted each other's lives considerably. I am so proud of the educator he is, but more so I am proud of the man he is and how he makes me want to be better every day.

A JOURNEY TO ENLIGHTENMENT
Bradlee W. Skinner

"It is truly amazing to see what can happen when you surround yourself with those who are determined to see you succeed and rid yourself of those who are hoping to see you fail. The same can happen for your students in your classroom. Believe in them. Tell them. Show them."
~Bradlee Skinner

In the vast education landscape, the classroom is a nucleus, a crucible where knowledge is forged, minds are shaped, and futures are molded. It is not merely a physical space bounded by four walls but a dynamic environment pulsating with the energy of curiosity, exploration, and discovery. With that in mind, I have never been one to find joy in the phrase Classroom Management. You see, I do not want to *manage* my students. I find the more accurate phrasing to be Classroom Leadership as leading our students is more what educators do. This shift empowers our students, allowing them to take ownership of their learning journey and foster a sense of responsibility.

If our focus is on the management of students, then rules, routines, and regulations within the walls of the room are what we spend more time repeating rather than learning. When the focus is on leading our students, relationships, culture, and climate take more time at the start of a school year, and the results are more learning throughout the year with fewer behavioral issues.

Traditionally, the classroom has been synonymous with rows of desks facing a teacher at the front, a layout reminiscent of the Industrial Revolution's assembly lines. However, as pedagogical paradigms evolve, so too does the physical configuration of the classroom. Years ago, I ditched the janitorial style of easy-to-clean rows for a flexible seating arrangement. I created collaborative workspaces, and added technology integration to redefine the traditional classroom, transforming it into a hub of innovation and creativity. This innovative approach has significantly increased student engagement, with my students expressing their love for a classroom that feels more like a bookstore or coffeeshop than a regular classroom. For upperclassmen at the high school level, having a space where every student can look their classmates in the eyes as they speak dramatically changed their behaviors and attitudes. This arrangement allows for deeper connections among students as they actively listen to the person they hear and see. It further limits inappropriate conversations and bullying as students tend to avoid snide comments when everyone can see each other, and they cannot hide at the back of the room or say something cruel behind someone's back.

Many outside of education currently view the words, diversity, equity, and inclusion as "four-letter words" with no place in school. However, I believe that to create the best classroom culture possible, we must recognize that our students come to us from varied backgrounds, cultures, and abilities. It is in our halls and our classrooms where these students converge, enriching the fabric of learning with their unique perspectives. Inclusivity is not merely a buzzword but a guiding principle, ensuring that every voice is heard, every mind is valued, and every learner is empowered to reach their full potential. By embracing diversity and inclusivity, we not only create a more harmonious learning environment but also prepare our students for the diverse world they will enter.

Within the classroom, the teacher assumes the role of a guide, a facilitator, and a mentor. Gone are the days of didactic instruction, replaced by inquiry-based approaches that encourage critical thinking, problem-solving, and self-directed learning. The teacher is no longer the sole purveyor of knowledge but a co-creator of learning experiences, scaffolding students' understanding and nurturing their intellectual curiosity. Building a classroom culture and climate that allows for self-discovery, mistake-making, improving, and learning from peers is far more effective than the antiquated sage-on-the-stage I was initially taught.

Central to the classroom experience is the notion of community. Beyond its academic function, the classroom serves as a microcosm of society, where students learn the values of empathy, respect, and cooperation. Students cultivate essential social and emotional skills through collaborative projects, group discussions, and peer interactions, laying the foundation for responsible citizenship and global engagement. I have found that each year, I spend less time on teaching the rules and regulations of my classroom because students come to my classroom more prepared with a previous understanding of my expectations. This comes only from students talking about their time in my class. The culture and climate within my room is a topic of discussion among students and is spoken of in a positive light. New students come to my room having already heard about lessons, learning, and expectations, and this allows me to build on those notions to create or strengthen relationships, which makes rules and regulations easier to accept when we get to those discussions.

The classroom is more than just a physical space; it is a sanctuary of learning, a catalyst for ideas, and a beacon of hope. This is what a positive classroom culture and climate can create for students. As we navigate the complexities of the educational landscape, let us remember that the classroom is not merely a destination but a journey toward enlightenment, empowerment, and transformation. It is this culture that allows me to embark on a learning journey with my students and embrace the boundless possibilities within the hallowed walls of the classroom, year after year.

Action Steps:
1. Explore flexible seating, like Mr. Skinner.
2. Step away from the sage-on-the-stage mentality.
3. Think of your classroom as a journey to empowerment and transformation.

Bradlee makes some very important points in this passage, but paramount to me is giving the space and permission to be flexible. I want to really point this out for school and district leaders. It is not easy to allow teachers the flexibility to create this unique learning space when the traditional model is what is typically favored. But is the traditional model really what's best for kids? We love to use that phrase, but our decisions don't always align with its reality. For teachers to create spaces where students feel included, where their voice is welcome, and where they can genuinely grow and thrive, leaders *must* trust teachers and give them the freedom they need to make it happen.

Similar to Bradlee's focus on creating spaces that are inclusive and build community, each teacher needs to find the clarity within themselves around what it is they want and are looking for in their classroom. Those who know me well know that one of my big topics, one I will bang the drum repeatedly for, is clarity. If we are not clear about what it is that we are looking for, what we want to see occurring in the building, the classroom, and in our school community, it becomes quite difficult to attain. To me, gaining clarity is much like setting goals. If you don't know what you want to achieve the odds are you won't achieve it.

But how do we gain that clarity in our classroom? I refer to balcony leadership in my book *Road to Awesome: The Journey of a Leader* as one important way to find your clarity. It was a visualization exercise for me, seeing in my mind's eye what was important to me, laid out on the basketball court that kept me focused and gave me space for self-reflection. In this next passage, Lindsay Titus shares another very powerful method for each of us to get clear about what we want and what we are looking for in our classroom.

Like so many others, my connection with Lindsay Titus began through an online connection, in her case the Teach Better community. Lindsay and I have visited many times over the past several years, primarily due to both of us being edupreneurs (you know, educator - entrepreneurs). We met in person in the fall of 2021 at the Teach Better conference and bonded further over both being dance parents (me now retired from the dance-dad world, Lindsay just getting warmed up) Lindsay is a true friend and an inspiring human being.

VISUALIZE THIS
Lindsay Titus
Elementary Educator, Author, Speaker

*"To define yourself, means to know yourself. To know yourself,
means to trust yourself. To trust yourself, means to love yourself.
To love yourself, means to honor yourself."*
~ Lindsay Titus

Whenever I am exploring a topic, an essential first step is to create awareness and understanding of what that topic is and what it means to me. That awareness becomes the driving force to creating long-lasting and impactful change. Without purposeful awareness, life can feel like we are living on a merry-go-round, taking various actions, but still just going in circles. As an educator who has served in many roles, from classroom teacher to behavior specialist to assistant principal, I have seen the importance of establishing, building, and strengthening a classroom culture over time by bringing awareness to the forefront through visualization.

Without awareness of what we desire, from both our and our students' perspectives, we run the risk of creating a classroom culture that isn't actually serving the community within it. This is why awareness is an essential part of the process. So, where do we begin? A simple visualization practice is all it takes to start building momentum to define a classroom culture that not only serves you as the educator you are, but also your students.

Here is a simple visualization practice to try:
- Close your eyes and take a deep breath. Give yourself permission to allow your mind to wander and get curious.
- Visualize your ideal classroom community.
- Pay close attention in your visualization to what it sounds like in your classroom. What do you hear? What words are being spoken?
- Now, focus on what it looks like in your classroom. Where are the students and

where are you? What are students doing? How are students treating one another?

- Next, explore what it feels like. When you stand in your ideal classroom, what feelings come forward?

- Within your exploration, reflect on how you want your students to experience you and their peers within this community. Explore how you want your students to experience their time and learning within the classroom.

Following your visualization, open your eyes, and write or draw as much as you can from your exploration. Here is the key to this practice and why it is so informative in the creation of classroom culture: classroom culture is the combination of a variety of practices that are essential to the growth and expansion of any classroom. These practices include instructional practices, restorative practices, social emotional practices, and behavior change practices all coming together to create a space that is authentic to the people within it. Being able to see these in our visualization, helps us make them a reality in our spaces.

Classroom culture doesn't come in a book or catalog. It isn't something that can be copied or artificially created. Classroom culture is an experience. It is unique and authentic to every individual that is part of the community. For this reason, your classroom culture will continue to expand throughout the year and every year after that. Classroom culture is not something to create in a day. It does not happen through passive passing of information. It is created and strengthened every day through intentional and purposeful interactions and practices that highlight the authenticity of everyone in the room.

The reason this visualization practice is so powerful in creating a transformative classroom culture, is that you can do it as often as you'd like and make adjustments as often as needed. It is a practice that involves your voice as well as your students', coming together to create a community for all.

Action Steps:
1. Complete the visualization exercise highlighted by Lindsay.
2. Try a visualization exercise with your students.
3. Be authentic in creating a positive space for kids.

There were many summer days spent standing in my empty classroom visualizing what I was hoping to see in the coming year. Yes, I was that teacher. The one who was back in their classroom as soon as the wax on the floor was dry. Visualizing your classroom space, your students at work, and what your environment will be like can be such a powerful exercise. But what if your students are not in your physical space? In nearly every state in the union, virtual schools have gained a considerable presence. Since the 2016-17 school year, the number of students attending full time virtual schools has more than doubled from just under 300,000 students to over 630,000 in the 2021-22 school year. This statistic alone drives the importance of developing classroom culture not only in physical classrooms but virtual ones as well. To share some insights into this work, we reached out to one of the very best virtual educators in the country, Baird Swedman.

I connected with Baird through his superintendent, Dr. Eric Nichols. Baird is the Silvies River Charter School Director of Student Success and teacher advocate. He has been a top notch teacher, teaching coach and all-around highly-effective educator. From rural practices to best practices in virtual instruction, Baird is a leader in the field.

COLLECTION OF CAMERAS
Baird Swedman, M.Ed
Western Oregon Dean of Students, Silvies River Charter School

"Education feeds the brain but nourishes the soul"
~Baird Swedman

It's easy to think that creating a classroom culture in the virtual world is substantially different than in an in-person classroom setting, but in reality, it isn't. Teachers that create effective classroom cultures connect with students and meet them where they are and at their level, and it doesn't matter if this happens in a classroom or through a computer screen. Students need to feel welcome and safe, comfortable but also vulnerable, and open to new learning experiences. Teachers that foster these feelings within their students are those that create a classroom culture that is positive, student-centered, and simply enjoyable.

There is always going to be an element of teacher authority present in a classroom or in the virtual world, but students must also feel as if their ideas, questions, and input are welcomed and accepted. Teachers and students are not equals in their knowledge of the subject matter or in their roles of managing a learning environment, but they are equals in that they bring meaningful contributions to the table and can enhance the learning experience. A teaching approach that envelopes this mentality will certainly create an effective classroom culture. When students feel seen, heard, appreciated, and valued, the learning opportunities are limitless, and it really doesn't matter if this happens together in a single classroom or as a collection of cameras on a computer screen.

Action Steps:
1. Reach out to your virtual students to make sure they feel seen.
2. Make sure your students and teachers feel heard.
3. Even virtually, make sure your space is safe.

In *Hacking Leadership*, Sanfelippo and Sinanis argue that all schools should be focusing on being student-centered. It is their position that students who feel safe are more confident, leading to students being primed for optimal learning. It is no secret that there is a tremendous teaching and learning benefit from having students working in a welcoming environment.

Throughout this chapter, the focus has been on creating spaces where our students feel safe and are included in not only the learning but in the way it takes place. As you continue to work toward developing the classroom culture where your students feel seen, heard, valued, and trusted, lean into the lessons from this chapter. Don't strive to manage your students, instead lead them and walk with them in their learning journey. Visualize what it is you wish to see in your classroom, and then create that culture where the cameras are on (in person or virtual) and students feel included, see themselves capable of success, and working to be the best they can be every day.

Reflection Questions:

1. Reflect on your own K-12 schooling. Did you have an experience as a student that either positively or negatively shaped your view of the classroom?
2. How are you creating spaces where students have a voice in the physical environment of the classroom?

3. Consider Lindsay's visualization exercise. What might be the benefit for you in doing this type of exercise on a regular basis? Would your students benefit from this exercise?
4. In the virtual environment, what are some steps similar to Baird's you can take to ensure your students are seen and heard regardless of the platform in which they learn?

Chapter Five Notes:

CHAPTER SIX

Student-Centered Practices that Engage

When I first walked into the classroom, roughly 15 minutes before students would come through the door, I found a two-page document sitting on the desk. It began something like, "Thank you for covering my classes today, I am hopeful you have a great day with my students. Here is everything you will need to know about my kids, the assignments, and our classroom procedures." As a substitute teacher, I always appreciated notes like these, as it wasn't always what I would see. Sometimes, I was left with just a simple lesson plan, instructions on how to cue up the video and hand out the guided notes or something of this nature. Yes, I was a substitute teacher prior to landing my first full-time teaching job. And I think it did a lot to prepare me for leading my own classroom full of kids. The truth is, leading a classroom can be intimidating, but only if we allow it to be. The keys are found in confidence and engagement.

What exactly does engagement mean? If we were to ask a dozen educators to define student engagement, would their answers be remotely close to each other? School leaders share with me frequently their goal of greater student engagement in the classroom. Yet many struggle to define what that actually is and how they might measure both it and its impact on student learning. In *School of Engagement*, Alsheimer defined engagement as students being completely absorbed in an activity and genuinely interested in what they are learning. Let's be honest, we have all been in classrooms (both as educators and as students) where time flew by, and we were totally engrossed in what we were doing. That is true engagement. For the purposes of this chapter, I would like to focus on three different levels of engagement: disengaged, compliant, and engaged.

Disengaged
"Bueller... Bueller... Bueller..." Thinking of disengaged classrooms, my mind cannot help but go to that hilarious scene in the economic teacher's classroom in the movie *Ferris Bueller's Day Off*. Students were actually drooling. He was so boring! While most classroom disengagement doesn't look quite like this, it is true that if you bore your students, you will certainly lose them. And with their technology right at their fingertips, you better bring your A-game every day.

Disengaged classrooms happen for a few different reasons, all of which are equally concerning. These reasons include but aren't limited to lack of teacher preparation, one-sided instruction (stand and deliver anyone?), tasks that are too easy/too complicated, and a lack of clear expectations and directions.

I was in a school recently where the levels of engagement were all over the place. In some classrooms, it was so low that I wondered if there were any expectations being held for the teachers and for that matter, expectations of the students. I learned that this school had been under the leadership of a principal who really just liked to make people happy. He avoided conflict at all costs, which allowed his teachers to make choices independent of any overarching goals the school might have been working toward. In several classrooms, students were on their phones, cruising YouTube videos, and unable to speak to what their learning objective was for the day. Teachers in these rooms did not seem overly concerned with off-task behaviors and worked with the students who wanted to learn. Man, I was so frustrated, and it wasn't even *my school*.

I sat down with the new principal, who I was hired to support, to have a conversation about what we were seeing in the classrooms of her building. She had been a teacher in the building for many years prior and had high expectations for student work in her classroom. She shared that she had no idea things had fallen this far in the school and wasn't sure where to begin. We started with a discussion around expectations.

When disengagement occurs in the classroom, it typically derives from a lack of expectation, an unclear expectation, or lack of support. I know in times when I have had low engagement in lessons, it came from me being a bit underprepared and unable to clearly articulate the purpose of a lesson or activity. As the teacher, if I am showing up this way, it is going to make for a long day.

How to fix it:
- Over prepare - this is a step that early career educators in particular can benefit from. If you've ever planned something and came up incredibly short of activities or

students completed work much more rapidly than you thought they would, you know what I am talking about. Ensure that you always have more, a backup plan or the next step in student learning, prepared and ready to go.

- Get them moving - when students are bored (and odds are you might be too) get them up, get them moving. Use some cooperative learning strategies, get them talking to each other, let them do the work.

- Add competition - nothing gets a room of kids going like a competition. Adding in review games, challenges, or scavenger hunts can jazz up nearly any boring lecture or lesson.

- Get clear - outline for yourself and for your students exactly what you are expecting of them for the lesson, the unit, etc. When students know the expectation, the likelihood they move toward it increases considerably. (** Administrators, this is key for your teachers too - if you aren't clear about what you expect of them, it is hard for them to hit the target.**)

- Listen to your students - if you are seeing disengagement (or it is shared with you in a classroom observation), consider asking your students how they would gauge their own levels of engagement. Helping students to be more self-aware can drive engagement levels up and increase student performance.

Compliant

If you are, or ever have been, a school administrator, you probably know what it is like to sit in a classroom and complete a formal teacher observation. I have lived through many different models of what should and should not be done during an observation from the administrator side of the desk. Whether you are scripting a full lesson or just taking a few notes, you've undoubtedly discovered students behaving differently with you in the room. Why is that? Typically, it is their desire not to make their teacher look bad in front of the boss. It comes from a place of compliance. Do what is expected because it is expected not because it's necessarily what you are wanting to do.

One of the schools I worked with faced a challenge that many other schools face, compliant students rather than engaged students. The distinction here is much like the example above. Students in this particular school mostly came to school on time, mostly got good grades, and mostly made good choices. In many cases, they came from families that had an expectation of their children to do well in school. That did not, however, always translate into students who were truly engaged with their learning. In this school, the challenge was taking students from a place of compliance to a place of true engagement.

I've written and spoken often about compliance. At one point in my career, I worked in a school and district that was really focused on ensuring that people and students were compliant with rules, regulations, and expectations. Now, don't get me wrong; I think people should be compliant with regulations and rules. However, when compliance is our goal, we tend to find engagement is quite low. Working in an environment that focuses on compliance, tends to result in people who don't take risks as they tend to be fearful of the consequences of failure.

What does compliance look like in our students? Compliant students are our students who are sometimes described as being good at the game of school. They will sit in their seats, take notes, complete assignments, and so forth. However, compliant students are not truly engrossed in their learning. Instead, they are doing what is expected of them more out of obligation than from their own desires. Compliant students learn sometimes in spite of us rather than because of us. At times, the compliant student becomes that way because we may not be challenging them, allowing them to express themselves, or express their learning, yet because of the circumstances, they play along.

Compliant students are often mislabeled as engaged in a classroom because they don't have the typical disengaged look about them. School leaders will identify them incorrectly in walkthrough observations because the student demonstrates compliance.

How to fix it:
- Find out what students want to learn about a topic or subject - as teachers, we sometimes move forward with the assumption that all students want to learn about a subject for the same reason. If we discover what our students' interests are and how they can be applied to our subject

area or topic, we have a greater opportunity to hook them into their learning.

- Consider project-based or problem-based learning - when students are prompted with a challenge or are given the opportunity to demonstrate their learning in their own way, the ownership of learning goes up dramatically. Now, take note here: I am not saying put them in a group and do the old group grade thing. I am talking about a true student-driven demonstration of their learning.

- Be collaborative as a staff - if you want to change the level of engagement from compliant to truly engaged, work together! Engagement is tough to define in the first place, so create a collective description, look-fors for school leaders and instructional coaches to provide feedback, and common language for staff and students to use to describe their learning.

- Consider the level of questioning in the classroom - when it comes to rigorous instruction, often we refer to Webb's Depth of Knowledge (DOK). When moving students to a high level of engagement, DOK is an important part of the equation. In particular, where a student is in terms of DOK can be determined through examining the type of questions being asked of them and what they are able to do with knowledge gained in the class as a result of that learning. Classrooms that have a high level of compliant students may consider examining the questions being asked by teachers and how they might challenge students to think more deeply, apply their knowledge, and transfer their learning to other applications.

Engaged

I received a lot of interesting requests as a high school principal. Some were just plain odd such as a group in the community that wanted our students to participate in a beard growing contest (can't make that up). Others were super rewarding, like our downtown coalition president meeting with me and creating an annual Tiger Town Bash to promote our fall activities and further integrate our community with our school. But one in particular stands out as the definition of student-owned demonstration of learning.

Every year, seniors in our Health Occupations Career Academy were charged with some type of culminating project. The project needed to make an impact on the community at large while incorporating what the students had learned from their job shadowing experiences as well as their presentation and speaking training. One particular senior, Colton, had been shadowing an EMT and ambulance service in town. Colton had actually been working as a licensed EMT while still going to high school. He approached me with an idea that, if I am being honest, I nearly said no to right away. Colton wanted to stage a mock drunk driving accident on our campus prior to the prom in the spring. While I applauded the idea, my first thought was *this is way too big of a project for a high school senior to take on*. The funny thing about students who really have a passion for what they are learning is they will surprise you with what they can accomplish.

Over the next couple of months, Colton was able to plan the entire experience (complete with a wrecked car rolled on its side). He had fellow seniors playing roles as victims, parents in attendance, firefighters, law enforcement, and an EMT crew. This was a true demonstration of his learning, and it had a strong impact on our community. Honestly, as I sit here typing this out there are tears in my eyes remembering the scene, our kids, and our families' faces.

Does a student have to recreate a DUI crash scene to be fully engaged? No, of course not. But just imagine what can happen in your school or your classroom if students are really immersed in their learning and excited to discover what comes next. You don't have to put on a show, you don't have to make everything a game, but finding a way to connect student's interests with the topics at hand does help move the engagement needle in the right direction.

Want an example from elementary school? As a superintendent, I pushed really hard to move our schools from compliant to engaged. We lived in a community where most of our kids were going to do well in school, regardless of what we did as educators. So, why not raise the stakes and challenge our students more? We did extensive research, including a trip where I took a number of staff members to visit several project-based learning (PBL) schools. My third grade team was one of the first grade levels to jump into work, focusing on their geography standards as the starting point. They created a project where students became travel guides and worked to sell their clients (they were all assigned one person from the community or school) on the location they selected. The amount of math, writing, speaking, and listening, not to mention geography the students learned was astounding. (My travel agent sold me on a wonderful trip to Detroit, Michigan - I was actually in Detroit later that year for a job fair and took some pictures for him - he loved it!)

I am not saying that we must use projects to increase engagement. Those are just two very good examples. If you've been in a room with students debating or discussing the motives of a novel character or even just seen the looks in the eyes of students fully enthralled in any activity, you know what I am trying to get at with this passage on engagement. We must continue to find ways to capture kids' attention, connect to their interests and passions, and tap into arenas they may not even have considered as interesting or thought provoking. It is in the engagement space where the true art and science of teaching, along with sometimes the performance aspect, really lies.

How to get it:
- Invest in relationships with students so you know where their interests and passions lie. Then find a way to tap into that whenever possible.
- Give genuine space to student voice, choice, and ability to share their learning their way.
- Investigate project-based learning if you have not already. It is a powerful method to engage students, give them agency, and for learning to truly stick.

Gamification stays relevant in school settings for a reason. Because it works. The video game industry is enormous; the sports industry is huge. Why? Competition sparks creativity; it sparks winning and losing. The adrenaline of the game is what fills arenas and fantasy football leagues and seasons year in and year out.

I've been married for over 20 years. Marriage isn't always easy, but I adore my husband. He is in his 40s, and he is never more excited than when he plays fantasy football. He spends hours talking about his strategy to win. He pulls our son in to play too. They pour over lineups and check stats. Not only are they trying to win, but they are bonding over it too. Our entire family does the exact same thing for March Madness. We fill out brackets; we check our points. My husband and son research for their brackets. My daughter and I pick teams based on if we like their mascots or not. More times than not, my daughter or myself will win the March Madness bracket. The best mascot schools seem to upset top seeds on a regular basis.

On Christmas day, after we've opened presents and eaten our cinnamon rolls we make once a year, we gather in the living room for games. Board Games, card games, trivia games, you name it, we play it. There we are in our matching pajamas from the night before competing in trivia teams and laughing and yelling and laughing some more. Why? Because it is fun, and when it is fun, people come! Tradition. Games. Music. Food.

Teams. Winning. Losing. Bonding. These are the types of environments that our students love too. I often provide professional development for secondary teachers, and I reiterate over and over again that we don't outgrow play, ever! These are little bitty kids trapped in great big bodies. They want to play, laugh, and have fun!

Engage in this chapter and get some ideas to put in your toolbelt for your staff and students today.

I first met Jacki through social media, like so many of our connections. But in the fall of 2022, I got to spend some time with her in person at the Teach Better Team conference in Akron, Ohio. We were just coming out of the covid funk, finally returning to in-person conferences and events. On the first evening, I drove a group of attendees to a social event, and in my rear view mirror was Jacki. I told her it was like Instagram came to life in my car. Her passion for life and for kids is amazing. Jacki is a true shining light in our beautiful profession.

TOOTHPASTE
Jacki Mjoen
Seventh Grade Math Teacher, IL

"The bravest thing we can do as educators to shape our classroom culture is to show up authentically. It's risky, vulnerable, and a bit scary, but when we do, it encourages our students to do the same. We want our kids to feel comfortable being themselves in our classrooms, but creating that kind of culture starts with us doing the same. When students see that we're human too – dealing with our own emotions and challenges – they learn from how we

navigate those moments. What we model has a way of coming back to us, often in surprising and beautiful ways." -
~Jacki Mjoen

"Toothpaste!" I hear one of my students shout from across the room. This means someone has said something that probably wasn't a good choice. My students will continue to say this to each other all year as they navigate learning how to work together. It's a word we use to communicate that what was said was hurtful and not okay. It's a word that will continue to reinforce the classroom culture long after the toothpaste demonstration.

"Did you bring your toothbrush to math today?" I ask the kids as I start unboxing the 99-cent toothpaste that no one ever buys. "This demonstration is sponsored by Aim." Eyes become big and spines tall as 28 faces stare at me with confusion and curiosity.

"Mrs. Mjoen, I already brushed my teeth."

"What are we doing?"

"Can I eat it?"

It's the first day of school in my seventh grade math classroom and things are about to get minty. I stand in front of my students with a paper plate and a popsicle stick. I begin to squeeze the toothpaste out of the tube, making a huge green minty pile on the paper plate. The classroom remains intrigued as I ask, "Who thinks they can get this toothpaste back into the tube?" Hands shoot up, and every year I have three eager students who try so hard but cannot get the toothpaste back into the tube.

Proud of their efforts, I return to the front of the room with the empty tube and plate full of toothpaste. While this was highly entertaining, and now our classroom smells like the dentist's office, there is a point to this. Just as the toothpaste could not be returned to the tube, the same is true with our words. Once they are out, we can not take them back. So, in this classroom, our words will encourage, uplift, and support one another. Math is hard and not everyone's favorite class. This needs to be a safe space for all of us to try and try again. We can't be successful in learning without people to lean on and lift us up. So, if I hear anything other than kind words, I will look at you and say *toothpaste,* and you will know exactly what I mean.

Toothpaste sets the tone for the rest of the year. It lays the groundwork upon which math learning can happen. It invites accountability to keep our learning environment one where failure isn't seen as being stupid or dumb but the first attempt in learning. Math has said a lot of things to my students before they even enter my room on that first day. For that reason, every year I make it a priority (regardless of the crazy first day schedules) to bring out the toothpaste and invite my students into a math classroom that has the potential to rewrite the math lies. Our math classrooms do not need more shame from the condemning words between students, or from the educator. You would be surprised at the impact a little toothpaste can make.

Action Steps:

1. Try Jacki's Toothpaste lesson.
2. How do you squash mean words in your class?
3. How do you make sure students don't feel shame during a difficult concept?

Not only does Jacki engage, but she teaches life-changing lessons that go beyond the classroom and stick with you for a lifetime. So, what are your life-changing lessons? What wisdom have you gathered that shapes the way you teach, lead, and inspire?

One of the most powerful forms of professional development isn't found in a book, a conference, or even a formal training - it's right down the hall. Your best resource is your fellow educators. Take the time to step into a colleague's classroom, especially one of your teacher besties. Watch them teach a lesson they're proud of. Observe their passion, their creativity, their connection with students. There is something truly transformative about seeing great teaching in action, and it can reignite your own love for the craft.

And here's the thing - positivity is contagious. Relentlessly promote it on your campus. Lift each other up. Celebrate the small wins. As educators, we face an overwhelming amount of negativity. The outside noise can be deafening - people who haven't set foot in a classroom in decades making laws about what we do every single day, critics who think teaching is easy simply because they were once students themselves. It's easy to let that negativity seep in, to let it weigh us down.

But we don't have to let it. We combat it by creating our own culture - one of encouragement, enthusiasm, and joy. We gas each other up. We find ways to make learning fun. We pour our energy into our students and into each other. We work hard, but we also smile, we laugh, and we make memories. Because when it's fun, the people will come. When we lead with passion, students engage. When we support one another, we thrive. So let's keep showing up, lifting each other higher, and doing the work that matters.

I had the great fortune to be Jessica Laverty's instructional coach a few years ago. Even as a brand new teacher, she was innately gifted with instructional practices and building relationships with her students. I loved going into her room and taking part in her class. It is my great privilege to bring you her words of wisdom.

BE ENGAGING, RELEVANT AND CARE ABOUT KIDS AS HUMAN BEINGS
Jessica Laverty
Middle School ELA Educator

*"I've learned that people will forget what you said, people will forget what you do, but people will never forget
how you made them feel."
~Maya Angelou*

A positive classroom climate goes hand in hand with having strong classroom management. It starts by having very clear expectations that are consistently followed by everyone in the room, including myself, so that students know we are in this together. While consistency is key, you must make sure to allow a little flexibility in case life gets in the way. I teach junior high students, so life gets messy sometimes, and they need to know that is okay.

Once the expectations are set, it is important to start building relationships and trying to make true connections. This can be accomplished by simply acknowledging a fresh, new haircut or attending extracurricular activities your students participate in. I have found that the simplest gestures and conversations end up having the biggest impact on my students because they know I genuinely care about them as people. Once they know you care, they are hooked, and they will do just about anything to make you proud.

I also believe you must have an engaging and relevant curriculum to have a positive classroom climate. I put a strong emphasis on teamwork and collaborative learning. It keeps them wanting to come to my class every day because I continually surprise them with interactive lessons that allow them to connect to the material and each other. My favorite back-to-school activity is a blindfolded puzzle competition. I skip the boring first-day-of-school syllabus review, and this activity sets the tone from day one that we are going to rely on each others' strengths to accomplish hard tasks throughout the year.

All of this, throw in some positive reinforcement, and even an occasional Jolly Rancher bribe and you are all set for a successful year full of growth.

Action Steps:
1. Utilize collaborative learning groups.
2. Use Jessica's blindfold puzzle competition to build community in your room.
3. Try some positive reinforcement.

Schools should feel like family - a place where students and staff alike feel valued, connected, and part of something bigger than themselves. When we cultivate a strong sense of community, we create an environment where students thrive, teachers are energized, and learning becomes an experience rather than just a task. But building that culture doesn't happen by accident; it takes intentionality, creativity, and a willingness to embrace new ideas.

So, as the lead learner in your building, how can you foster a sense of camaraderie, belonging, and engagement? One of the most effective ways is through community competitions - activities that bring students, staff, and even parents together in a shared experience of fun, teamwork, and school spirit. Imagine the energy in your building when students and teachers face off in a high-stakes dodgeball game, or when hallways buzz with excitement over a school-wide talent show. What about a Hallway Coin Challenge, where different grades compete to raise money for a local charity? Or an all-out battle for the most creative Black History Month door decorations? These moments build memories, strengthen relationships, and make school a place where students and staff want to be.

It doesn't stop at the school level. Teachers can transform their own classrooms into engaging, game-like environments. Some educators have revolutionized learning by allowing students to "level up" with points instead of traditional grades - though most gradebooks aren't built that way just yet. But there are still countless ways to gamify instruction and infuse play into learning. Imagine students competing in a Rock, Paper, Scissors tournament to determine who presents first, or engaging in a heated debate judged by local community leaders. Picture a classroom buzzing with excitement during a Socratic Seminar or Speed Discussion, or the pride students feel when they create their own companies, participate in a mock job fair, and receive written offer letters. From Academic Team vs. Teacher trivia battles to student-led TED Talks, the possibilities for competition and engagement are endless.

Culture isn't built in a day – it's built every day. If you want to see change in your building, don't wait for it to happen. Go out and find schools that have the culture you admire, learn from them, and bring those ideas back. Shift the mindset from these are *my* students to these are *our* students. Be present. Walk the hallways, sit with students at lunch, show up to extracurriculars, and be an active part of the learning experience. Surround yourself with innovators, empower them to lead, and create a culture where positivity is louder than negativity.

Where do we start? We start here. We start now. We build the schools our students deserve – together.

Chelsea Blackburn is the definition of a highly sought-after teacher. Both of my kids, along with nearly every other child at

their school, wanted to be in Ms. Blackburn's class. She brings an incredible amount of fun to her classroom, all while maintaining excellent control and holding her students to the highest standards. She's a once-in-a-lifetime educator, the kind that students remember long after they've left her class. Take a look at how she transforms her classroom into a close-knit family.

CLASS BUILDING, CONSISTENCY, AND CHOICE
Chelsea Blackburn, M. Ed.
Fifth Grade Math, Great Expectations Trainer

"When students feel valued and understood by their teachers, it creates a foundation of trust that encourages engagement and learning. Elements of consistency and choice

nurture a classroom atmosphere where students are not only ready to learn but are also invested in their own educational journey."
~Chelsea Blackburn

As the old expression goes, "You never get a second chance to make a first impression." You also never get a second chance to have a first day of school. Once supplies are collected and necessary procedures have been covered, I immediately get students out of their seats for my favorite class building activity, Blobs and Lines. Students work together to get into either an organized line or group based on a category I've given them - alphabetically by first name, favorite season, etc. While my students are completing these tasks, I attempt to stay as removed as possible and just simply observe. Personality types shine through with these activities. Once students feel they have themselves organized, each student shares their attributes so that commonalities and differences can be recognized. I always share where I would fit in to start reaching common ground with them as well. In the first weeks of school I invest a large chunk of my class time on several different class building activities, all with a common goal to establish a positive, caring environment.

This investment of time in class building is an essential part of my classroom management. A student's sense of belonging is a basic self-esteem need, so the quicker I can establish that they are an integral part of our class community, the faster I can begin to build trust. As a student's trust is built, I speak frequently about my expectations and my belief that they will all be successful and grow in their math abilities. I work hard daily to establish a caring relationship with each student to ensure that as mistakes are made, a student never doubts my love for them. They understand that behavioral or academic mistakes are a part of learning, and I'm simply trying to help them be successful.

Another pillar of my classroom management is consistency. Procedures are explained, demonstrated, and practiced. The fidelity I expect in procedures from my students is unrelenting. If a procedure isn't being followed, it's not a call for punishment – it demonstrates a need for that procedure to be practiced. Students don't enter the room as expected? Out the door we all go to practice. An environment where students know what is expected of them and what to expect is safe. A safe classroom puts a student's brain in the proper space to take in new information and one in which the student is more apt to take risks.

Providing my students with choice is the final piece that sets my classroom apart. When you sit back and think about how much of a student's school day is dictated to them, it's easy to see why they are so eager to have some autonomy in how they spend their time and demonstrate their knowledge. A daily element of choice in my classroom is the "I'm Through; What Can I Do?" board which provides choices for students to work through when they've finished the day's task. At the conclusion of units, I give students a tic-tac-toe board of activities to work through to prepare for tests. Free Choice Friday is a loved day in math class for my students. As I pull small groups for reteaching, my students have two to four activities to choose from to practice our skills from the week. My students appreciate this power of choice which only enhances our positive classroom environment.

Classroom management is an ever-evolving aspect of a successful classroom. The investment in class building, consistency provided by the educator, and power of choice provided to students can be very impactful in improving not only classroom management but also a positive classroom environment students are excited to be a part of.

Action Steps:
1. Think of your best classroom culture team-building activities. Can you use Chelsea's?
2. Put procedures in place, and be unrelenting about safety in your class.
3. Be consistent; kids deserve a safe space to call their own.

I will stand by this until the end of time: "Life is fun; learning should most definitely be fun!" Education is not meant to be dull, rigid, or uninspiring. It should be an adventure, a journey filled with moments of joy, curiosity, and excitement. When we create spaces where students love to learn, we cultivate a culture where engagement thrives, creativity flourishes, and lifelong learners are born.

I believe wholeheartedly in the power of finding joy in the education process. Learning should spark something deep within our students, something that keeps them coming back for more - not just because they have to but because they want to. Engaging our learners, our students, our kids is paramount to all of our success. When students are emotionally connected to what they are learning, when they feel seen, valued, and excited to participate, their potential is limitless. We are not just teaching content; we are shaping experiences, fostering confidence, and creating a love of learning that will carry them beyond our classrooms.

Some of the most powerful moments in education aren't found in test scores, assessments, or perfectly aligned lesson plans. They are found in the in-between moments: the shared laughter over a classroom game of Jeopardy, the energy of a spontaneous dance-off, the pride in sinking the winning free throw, the thrill of friendly competition to see who can create the best drawing in art class. These moments become core memories, not just for our students, but for us as educators. They remind us why we chose this profession in the first place.

Learning should feel alive. It should be immersive, dynamic, and filled with moments of joy. It's in the way a classroom comes together to cheer on a peer, in the excitement of tackling a new challenge, and in the simple moments of connection between teacher and student. It's about turning ordinary days into extraordinary ones.

So, let's start today. Let's lean into the power of joy, of creativity, of shared experiences. Let's make learning something our students look forward to. Because when we bring energy, when we bring fun, when we create a classroom culture that values happiness just as much as achievement, we set the stage for something truly incredible.

Let's make learning an experience they will never forget. Let's make it fun.

Reflection Questions:

1. Do you agree with Katie's sentiments about fun learning environments?
2. Should we constantly be trying to gamify our schools and classrooms?
3. Talk as a group about what you do at your school that creates a fun and competitive atmosphere.
4. Talk as a group about what you did as a kid that made your school environments fun.

Chapter Six Notes:

_____
_____
_____
_____
_____
_____
_____
_____
_____
_____
_____
_____
_____
_____

CHAPTER SEVEN

Trauma-Informed Practices for Healing and Growth

Throughout my career as an educator, I've had the opportunity to work across two different districts, in four distinct schools, and with a staggering twenty-eight different principals and assistant principals. That's twenty-eight unique leadership styles, twenty-eight distinct personalities, and twenty-eight diverse perspectives from which I've learned. Some leaders showed me how to lead effectively, and some showed me how not to. That is just the name of the education game. The school where I spent most of my career as an eighth-grade English teacher was a place where I found a supportive community, teacher besties, and worked with some administrators who genuinely cared about both students and staff as a family should. This school also served the district's highest-need student population.

The students at my beloved school came from what was, statistically, the third most violent neighborhood in our urban city. But don't get it wrong – my students were intelligent, capable, and often faced the challenges of generational poverty, where education was their best chance for a better future. As their teachers, we understood this and fully embraced it. However, at times, the violence that was all too common in their neighborhoods would occasionally spill over into the school.

It was February, and you have to know that by the second semester of school, I have a family classroom. We've been through some emotional lessons, we've laughed, cried, and had a lot of fun. My students know my expectations are high and that I love each and every one of them. This particular year, we had a kid named Drake. Drake came from extreme poverty. Sometimes, he found himself in homeless situations. He even wrote about how his dad didn't pay the rent for their apartment, so they were sleeping in a broken down car. It got so cold that the apartment manager allowed Drake and his two younger sisters to sleep in the lobby of the apartment complex until his dad could pay the rent again. He would come early to school to shower in the boys locker room and eat breakfast. As the adults in the building, we knew his circumstance and often helped him and his sisters with food, new clothes, and blankets as needed. His dad loved him dearly, and did as many jobs as he could to help pay for the apartment and utilities.

Drake would sleep in class sometimes, and I'd let him because I knew his story and so did our team. We must always know the stories of our kids and coworkers. That is how we build a family classroom and a family school. I was full of grace when it came to Drake and many kids like him. I would tutor him and others, let them redo a million assignments, and sit with them and help them on their journeys to further their education. Drake didn't allow the tough life he led to keep him from letting his sweet personality and big ole heart shine through. He could have very easily been hardened by the circumstances he found himself in, but he didn't. He was absolutely precious.

Not only was he a great kid, he was an amazing basketball player. At 6'4 in only seventh grade, he was the only kid in our district who could dunk at the age of twelve. We would marvel at him as he palmed that orange ball and jumped over half his teammates to dunk in our middle school gym. His dad believed he could get their entire family out of poverty if Drake could play basketball in college, so we all doubled down to help make that dream a reality.

But on this February morning at my cherished school, Drake ran in to tell us that something was brewing in the neighborhood and that we should be careful. He said seven fights were planned throughout the day, one by the tornado shelters, one under the bleachers in the gym, two outside, and on he rattled about what was planned. He told us some of the parents in the neighborhood followed kids to their bus stop and started fights there. We immediately reported it to our administration at the time and were told that kids were silly and the day would be fine; it wasn't. Drake was not listened to; we were not listened to. All of the fights that Drake said would happen, did. By the end of the day, we were exhausted from keeping our heads on a swivel and breaking up numerous brawls. I heaved a sigh of relief when the bell rang for the last class of the day. I looked up when all of a sudden, some of my students including Drake were racing for my room, and behind them a mob of other kids, who were not my students, were after them.

"Ms. Kinder," Drake yelled, "help!" To staunch the chaos, we had staggered our releases from class, so I happened to be the only adult in the vicinity. I held the door open for my students and started to push it shut when the mob of kids trying to fight Drake and friends began trying to bring my door down. Drake and I pushed against the door to finally get it shut. We sat in our community circle journaling our thoughts as I called, texted, and emailed the office to no avail. After school, parents gathered in the parking lot to fight. Police were called, arrests were made, ambulances circled the property, and our new principal, who had only had the head job for seven months, resigned that day.

Why is this story important, and why would I share it with you? Well, sometimes as leaders, as teachers, as principals, we need to listen to our people, our students, our staff. We can't shrug off a report of violence because we think it might not happen. If we have fostered this family culture in our schools, then our people need to be heard. Although I only worked for that certain principal for seven months, I learned a lot about leadership from her; how not to be. After she left, we got a principal who stayed for six years, one of the best in the business to this day. He listened, he observed, he was a servant leader for all to see.

Oh, and Drake... Well, Drake got a full ride basketball scholarship to a division two school where his dad and sisters also moved to live in campus housing because of a hardship scholarship that we helped Drake apply for. So, when it comes to teaching and the effect we can have on a school building, a family, a community, use grace over grades, see people over data, and know the stories of your students. You may be the only thread tethering them to goodness, to success, to safety.

I sat in the front row of a conference with my arms crossed waiting for the keynote to begin. Because I study the speaking game, my expectations for a keynote are high; I've seen the best in the business, and continue to study the game. "Who is this Stacy Nation?" I thought to myself. Stacy stepped on stage, and I was immediately mesmerized. She was thoughtful, hilarious, and real; the best kind of opening keynote, in my opinion. Before long, I was on my feet applauding wishing I could listen to her all day. And, of course, I love a powerful, funny, and impactful female speaker. Enjoy these words by the one and only, Stacy Nation. And my hope is that you one day get to see her live on stage.

HEALING TRAUMA THROUGH SCIENCE-BASED CLASSROOM STRATEGIES
Stacy G. Nation
LCSW, Clinician, Consultant, Speaker, Trainer, Author

"Go Be You. There is only one you, and only one you can do what you're here on this planet to do!"
~Stacy G. Nation

A woman left me a voicemail stating, "Please call me back. I need to get an appointment with you as soon as possible. My daughter's psychiatrist will no longer prescribe any medication without us meeting with you first."

I listened to the voicemail knowing full well that this woman called out of desperation. I called her back. She answered immediately and shared, "I don't know what to do anymore, and without these medications, I am sure that someone will die. You see, my daughter is actually a kinship placement, and she wakes up with terrible night terrors. She runs away. She threatens to kill us. She can no longer be in public school because she attacked everyone there. Please, please, meet with me for an hour so that I can get these medications." We set up an appointment. I told her we would meet for 60 minutes, but I blocked out three hours.

The day came, and the woman, her husband, and her daughter were sitting in my waiting room early. I brought them back to my office. The young girl, maybe eight at the time, sat on the floor, on her knees, with her shoulders bunched up to her ears. The parents sat in separate chairs. I sat on the floor, parallel to the young lady, and introduced myself. As I introduced myself, I took my heart rate with an oximeter and then explained what that was to the three of them. I took mom's heart rate. Then, dad's. Finally, the girl's. The girl's heart rate, as she sat, frozen, on her knees with her shoulders bunched up to her ears, was 128 beats per minute. She was terrified.

Thus, began a lifelong relationship with this family where we learned, discussed, and healed this young lady's trauma. The educators in her life played a critical role. The lessons in this story are vital for educators, parents, caregivers, and clinicians to understand. We cannot just focus on *behaviors*, we have to look at the *roots* of the behavior, and we have science to help us out. (Note: medication often assists with the behaviors, not the roots.)

We cannot fight physiology

The needs of our body will always win over reasoning and "behaving appropriately." This means that teachers can get familiar with how our nervous systems respond to stress, how students' behavior can be communicating their fight/flight/freeze response to classroom situations, and what we can do to turn things around. In the situation above, I spent time with the family teaching them about the reptile brain; the part of the brain that protects us. This young lady had a tremendous amount of trauma before she came to live with these parents. Her brain has literally been wired to protect her.

So, her threats, attacks, and words were keeping people away from her so that she could stay alive. Once the adults started to understand this stress response, we could start shifting the child's response. We started to collect data about heart rates, calorie intake, and sleep. Teachers can see that students can look "normal" on the outside, but they may be in crisis on the inside. This young lady's heart rate was well above what a resting heart rate should be (60-80 bpm). This one piece of information can help guide us to where we need to go to support our students.

Meet basic needs

When someone lives in a constant stressed out state, basic needs become wonky. A person may need more food so they can have more calories because they may be burning more calories due to a higher heart rate. A person may need a higher water intake because their brain is using lots of brain power to keep them alive. They also need more movement, more sleep, and possibly more (or less) touch, depending on their uniquely wired nervous system. Teachers who are curious about basic needs and unique sensory systems will be more equipped to find the ROOTS of behaviors.

Historically, schools have not intentionally focused on meeting basic needs prior to curricula. Now, with research and science, we know that basic needs MUST be met before a student can learn. Creating spaces and procedures for students to meet basic needs appropriately can be woven into the fabric of education for students in today's world.

Movement and play are basic needs

As we navigated 2020, we became very familiar with the importance of movement and play for ALL of us. As screens have become more ingrained in our lives, we see a decrease in movement and play. This decrease is impacting our overall health which also impacts the overall brain development of students. As teachers incorporate more movement and more play, we see an increase in learning and engagement. We also see that students with the highest levels of trauma NEED movement and play to function at their best.

Focus on relationships

No one wants to work harder for a boss they do not like. Students are the same. Get to know your students. Where do they come from? What do they love to do? What are their strengths? Building a safe, connected, loving relationship with the toughest student can turn behavior around and change the dynamics in your classroom.

As you continue in your career, I am sending you a huge thank you filled with LOVE! These science-based strategies are strategies for you too. Please take care of your physiology, meet your basic needs (seriously, please go to the bathroom during the day!), move your body, get out and play, and focus on your own relationships. These are HUMAN strategies, not just student strategies. Thanks for all you do!

Action Steps:
1. Immerse yourself in therapeutic and brain research, so you can better understand your students.
2. Know that movement and play are basic human needs, and we must incorporate them into class each day.
3. Find the stories of your students and they will be forever grateful for the work you put in to know them.

Sometimes, as educators, it feels like we are up against the world. A lot of the time, I believe the reason our kids feel lonely and isolated is because of the overuse of technology not only at home but in our schools too. My friend Kevin Honeycutt says, *"Our kids are growing up in a digital playground, and no one is on recess duty!"* Isn't that scary? But as teachers, we can be on the front lines of changing this for our students. We have seen that less screen time, not more, is beneficial to our students. We have seen their brain scans, we have seen what it has done to their mental health, so it is time we set up some boundaries in our schools and do what is best for kids in this arena.

This digital age in which our kids spend on average seven to ten hours a day interacting with some sort of screen, we must be vigilant in our pursuit to teach them humanity as well as how to be tech savvy. It isn't an easy feat, but with procedures in place, and engaging lessons planned, as teachers, we can band together and do what often seems impossible.

It is all about having balance in your schools and classrooms. Post-pandemic teaching has almost every school district with a one-to-one device policy for students. Meaning all kids have access to a school-issued device in case of inevitable, virtual days. This also means we can ban the cell phones in our classrooms. They don't need them for educational purposes.

Have team, classroom, and school procedures in place surrounding the phones. Of course our kids have phones, it is 2025. I'm not unreasonable. I give a student a warning to put them up, or I allow a frantic kid to call/text home if they are worried about something serious.

Images of a child's brain on a screen looks the exact way a drug addict's brain scans. It is about teaching our kids balance. Also, when phones are not present in the classroom - without the ever-present notifications and digital distractions - our kids learn better. If students even have their phones on their desks turned upside down, education research shows that their IQ is still lowered by ten points because of how distracting their phones are, buzzing every 30 seconds diverting their attention from the matter at hand - learning. Goodness, that is the antithesis of our mission in educating kids. That also means, you, as the educator, have to put yours up too. Be present with the babies sitting in front of you each day.

Create team/school procedures around school-issued devices. This could include a time limit with screens in each class. What is the consequence when a student decides to use their device for something inappropriate and not school related? It is so much easier to enforce procedures when everyone is on board. That includes superintendents, principals, instructional coaches, teachers, teacher assistants, substitutes, and parents.

Always have a back up, non-digital assignment in your back pocket for the kid who forgot their device at home, the kid who lost their privilege of having one, and any other foreseeable issues. The day you have planned an amazing digital lesson, you know the electricity and the wifi will be out. That is just how it goes.

Teach your students how to speak to one another in a professional manner. They are coming to us without the ability to communicate properly. A skill we must teach, as educators, is how to disagree and discuss topics in an educated and useful way. Utilize the Socratic Seminar, and utilize it often.

Teach students how to spot bias in their research, how to properly use a cool, gamey app, and how to create and collaborate using technology and artificial intelligence. However, don't just throw a worksheet on an iPad or a Chromebook. That isn't innovative; that is a worksheet on an iPad or a Chromebook. Might as well give them the assignment on paper because research shows that when people write pen to paper, they store it in long term memory unlike if they type.

Embed both technology and humanity in your lessons. Teaching our kids about how to have balance between these worlds, in both worlds, in life is paramount to their success, mental wellness, and happiness. Balance in my classroom might look like this: Split the class into debate teams, one side is pro, the other side con. They get 20 minutes to research with their teams for their sides. Reputable sources, strong debate points, and kindness above all else reigns in my room. Then, the tech goes away, and the debate is on. I like to get my kids up and moving in a four-corners debate.

It isn't easy, and it will not always be perfect. Doing what is relentlessly right for kids IS having high expectations for them, but it is also knowing that this career is human and messy at times. Educators, sometimes as we continue on our journey together, it is important to find ways to connect with each other, with kids, and help them connect to one another. We are made for connection, and we may be the only thread keeping some of our children from deep, isolating loneliness. In ten years, in fifty, your face will pop up in the minds of students as a person who helped them get through, a person who cared enough to walk beside them in moments of both hardship and happiness. That is never something we should take lightly.

Dr. Chris Culver is world class! He is passionate and purposeful in his work regarding Gen Z and Generation Alpha. A phenomenal speaker, friend, and person, Chris relates to his audiences all over the nation. Read his words on navigating and helping Gen Z with their well-being and be better for it!

NAVIGATING THE GEN Z PARADOX: BALANCING DIGITAL FLUENCY WITH EMOTIONAL WELL-BEING
Dr. Chris Culver
Gen Z specialist, Educator, Speaker

"Teachers and students thrive in relationships deeply rooted in trust – where they feel

empowered, have autonomy, and are valued for their contributions to the organization. Let's prioritize connection by offering our full attention, our most precious gift, and leading with empathy. When we treat others the way we wish to be treated, we create a ripple effect of kindness that leads to success for all."
~ Dr. Christopher S. Culver

There is no doubt that the students we serve today have vastly different needs than our students of just a few years ago. Today, our students show us that they need something in a variety of ways, even in ways we don't always understand. To best meet their needs, we have to seek to understand who they are and how they live and contribute to our society.

Our Gen Zers are a unique generation that require us, as educators, to understand them to ensure that we can not only reach them but can also teach them. I spent some time in the research to adequately understand our Generation Z, not only to be a better college professor but also ensure I can support teachers and leaders with our Gen Z student and teacher populations. Thank you Tim Elmore for writing the book, *Generation Z Unfiltered*.

Gen Z was born into a world saturated with smartphones and social media, and they possess an innate fluency in navigating the digital world. Yet beneath the surface lies a complex understanding of anxieties and mental health struggles, making their journey through life full of challenges and contradictions.

In my exploration of understanding motivation and school culture as it relates to teacher retention within the field of education, I found many parallels between teacher and student desires in relation to school culture, leadership, and fostering a space of belonging.

Today, people want to ensure they are part of spaces that foster relationships deeply rooted in trust where they have empowerment and autonomy but are also recognized for the value they add to the space – this is especially true for our Gen Z folks. They want to be seen, heard, valued, and respected. They want to have a sense of belonging.

To effectively engage with these individuals, we must harness multimedia elements into lessons to help foster a sense of digital literacy skills, but we must also help educate our Gen Zers on how to effectively use technology in a responsible way. As educators, we have to harness the power of platforms like Snapchat and Instagram as tools for connection and education. By incorporating multimedia elements into lessons and fostering digital literacy skills, educators can bridge the gap between traditional pedagogy and Gen Z's digital native mindset.However, the paradox of Gen Z extends beyond their digital fluency, encompassing a myriad of socio-emotional challenges. Despite their unparalleled access to information and resources, Gen Zers grapple with unprecedented levels of anxiety and mental health issues.

As educators, it is imperative we address these challenges head-on, providing a supportive environment where students feel empowered to seek help and advocate for their well-being. I believe adults are the dealers of hope and belief, and our Gen Zers need that more than ever.

How do we reach them? Well, these nine key areas can help make a meaningful difference in the lives of our Gen Zers.

Empowerment without Wisdom
Equipping Gen Z with digital tools and platforms is crucial, but it must be accompanied by the wisdom and critical thinking skills

necessary to navigate the complexities of the digital world responsibly. The BIG IDEA strategy involves providing a comprehensive approach to learning, incorporating various instructional methods to ensure deep understanding. It begins with instruction, where teachers furnish students with both knowledge and understanding through engaging lessons that utilize images and metaphors to summarize concepts. This is followed by demonstration, where students observe or practice the concepts they are learning, solidifying their understanding. Learning is not complete until students actually experience the insight for themselves, turning theory into practice through hands-on opportunities. Finally, assessment allows for ongoing evaluation and feedback, ensuring students gain helpful insights from their practices and receive guidance for improvement. This not only empowers students but creates wise students. This is not just a good practice for Gen Z students but really for all students.

Stimulation without Ownership

Providing engaging content and experiences is important, but it should not foster a culture of passivity. Gen Z must be encouraged to take ownership of their learning journey and actively engage with the material. Collaboration fosters ownership by encouraging group participation and collaborative learning, allowing students to talk with one another and share ideas. When there is an opportunity to embed play into the learning process, it is highly beneficial as it emphasizes the importance of interactive and exploratory learning, where students develop language and executive functioning skills, negotiate with others, and learn to manage stress.

The PROVE it method empowers students by guiding them through a problem-solving process: identifying the problem, building relationships through connecting and sparring with others, taking ownership of the solution, engaging with visuals to stimulate imagination, and gaining experience through hands-on learning projects.

This approach allows students to take ownership of their learning and creates shared learning experiences. This type of student experience takes high levels of trust because of the vulnerability required. Helping students feel safe within the space will allow for high levels of vulnerability which will yield high levels of trust - the foundation for an incredible learning experience for all.

Privileges without Responsibility

Gen Z students are inundated with messages and notifications from their devices – they live in a very digital world and at a faster rate than previous generations can adapt. This has led to a sense of instant gratification and lack of accountability which creates high levels of entitlement. Therefore, we have to help educate our Gen Zers on the appropriate ways to use technology.

Educators must instill a sense of accountability and ethical decision-making in their students' digital interactions. We have to break the shackles of entitlement by cultivating gratitude, teaching students to appreciate the privileges they have and to express gratitude for them. Building time for stillness and quietness allows students to reflect on their blessings and develop a sense of gratitude. Using gratitude as a meeting opener or class opening activity encourages students to express appreciation for one another and for the opportunities they have. This not only encourages students to be mindful of their actions, but also encourages accountability.

Involvement without Boundaries

Encouraging Gen Z to participate in various activities and initiatives is beneficial, but it must be balanced with clear boundaries to ensure their well-being and prevent burnout. Our Gen Zers do not have a lot of quiet time as they are constantly on their devices. They also have a Fear Of Missing Out (FOMO). We have to help our students focus on one-task at a time to help prevent burnout and improve or maintain mental health.

Empowering students to practice mindfulness, which helps alleviate depression, anxiety, and pain by focusing on the present moment positively improves students' mental health. Helping students develop coping skills and routines, such as identifying triggers, naming emotions, and practicing breathing exercises, equips students with tools to manage stress and maintain balance within their personal and academic life. Utilizing strengths for the greater good empowers students to channel their abilities into positive actions, such as solving problems and serving others.

Individualism without Perspective
Celebrating individuality is important, but it must be accompanied by an understanding of diverse perspectives and experiences to foster empathy and inclusivity. Helping Gen Z understand their virtues involves reflecting on their values and actions. Writing their own

eulogy prompts students to consider how they want to be remembered and what qualities they want to embody. Listing actions that align with their virtues helps students identify behaviors that demonstrate their values in action. Putting their actions into practice allows students to live out their values and make a positive impact on others. Holding each other accountable reinforces the importance of integrity and encourages students to support one another on their journey of personal growth. This allows students to foster a sense of community among their peers and teachers. Collectively, the focused work helps create a sense of community among everyone by having high expectations for themselves and others and by being held accountable for those actions and expectations.

Accessibility without Accountability
Making resources and support readily available is essential, but it must be coupled with accountability to ensure that students are actively engaging with the support provided. Helping students practice values such as honesty, discipline, respect, work ethic, and empathy involves incorporating activities that reinforce these principles into daily routines. Practicing activities like "Walk In Their Shoes" encourages students to consider the

perspectives of others and develop empathy for their experiences.

Fluidity without Integrity

Embracing change and adaptation is necessary in a fast-paced digital world, but it must be grounded in integrity and ethical values to maintain trust and credibility. Fostering character, responsibility, and self-control involves modeling integrity and ethical behavior in all aspects of life. Providing opportunities for students to practice decision-making and problem-solving in real-world situations helps them develop the skills and confidence to navigate such situations with integrity. I remember in my high school English class we would write our course syllabus, together, on the first day of school. This practice allowed us to hold each other accountable for meeting the expectations we set for ourselves. Today, I use the same practice in my college classroom, asking students to identify the norms and expectations for our time together in the learning space. When students have a sense of ownership in the space, it cultivates a sense of community and fosters a positive learning environment for all.

Opportunity without Resilience

Providing opportunities for growth and success is valuable, but it must be paired with the resilience to overcome challenges and setbacks along the way. Speaking words of belief and offering support and boundaries help students build resilience and develop a growth mindset. Encouraging students to set goals, pursue their passions, and persevere in the face of adversity fosters resilience, empowering them to overcome obstacles on their journey to success.

Research suggests that trust is built fastest between students and adults when students resolve their differences among one another through peer mediation. As a middle school administrator, I would implement an activity for conflict resolution where students wrote affirmations about themselves. This activity not only helped de-escalate students but also instilled belief in them and encouraged them to find common ground with each other. This activity not only fostered positive relationships among students but also provided an opportunity for everyone, including myself, to practice resilience.

Consumption without Reflection

Encouraging Gen Z to consume information and media is inevitable, but it must be accompanied by opportunities for reflection and critical analysis to promote deeper understanding and learning. Fostering critical thinking through experiential learning and emphasizing empathy as the starting point for learning promotes reflection and autonomy in Gen Z's learning journey. Creating experiences that begin with empathy and end with problem-solving helps students develop the skills to navigate complex issues and make informed decisions. Be bold in encouraging students to navigate complex issues – they are our future leaders!

Ultimately, the key to supporting Gen Z lies in fostering a culture of empathy, understanding, and empowerment. Educators can create a learning environment where Gen Z feels valued, supported, and equipped to thrive in an increasingly complex world by embracing their paradoxical existence and addressing their unique needs. We do this by creating relationships deeply rooted in trust. Here, students are empowered to be creative and innovative, have autonomy to take risks, and then we, as educators, recognize them for the value and contribution they make to our learning spaces. This not only fosters high levels of motivation but also creates a dynamic classroom environment rooted in trust, where all students feel seen, heard, valued, and respected.

To reach and teach our students, we have to know them. We do that by asking questions, listening and engaging with them, and seeking to understand.

Thanks for answering the call to serve, and thanks for all that you do for our students – you're a difference-maker!

I appreciate you and I am grateful for you! Keep shining, friends!

Action Steps:
1. Help your students navigate the in-person learning environment coupled with their digital tools.
2. Help your students cultivate gratitude.
3. Teach students to become more resilient.

Healing and growth are not one-time events; they are continuous journeys that require effort, reflection, and intentionality. As educators, leaders, and mentors, we dedicate so much of ourselves to nurturing, guiding, and shaping the minds and hearts of our students. But in the midst of pouring into others, we often forget a crucial truth; **we cannot give our best to our students if we are running on empty.** Taking care of ourselves is not selfish; it is necessary. If we are to model resilience, empathy, and emotional intelligence, we must first embody those qualities within ourselves.

We are more than just teachers, administrators, and mentors. We are human beings with emotions, struggles, and needs of our own. The weight of the work we do can be heavy - balancing lesson plans, grading, meetings, parent concerns, and the endless expectations placed upon us. The emotional labor of supporting students through their own challenges whether academic, social, or personal adds another layer of responsibility. And while we willingly take on this role, we must recognize that our well-being matters too.

We cannot effectively teach students how to navigate the complexities of life, how to interact with kindness, and how to take care of their own mental and emotional well-being if we are neglecting our own. If we are exhausted, burned out, or disconnected from ourselves, that energy spills over into our classrooms. Students notice. They feel it. They absorb the environment we create. That is why self-care is not an afterthought; it is an essential part of being an effective educator and a healthy human being.

Loving ourselves, our minds, our bodies, our hearts, means setting boundaries when we need them. It means giving ourselves permission to rest, to recharge, and to step away when necessary. It means allowing ourselves grace when we make mistakes just as we extend grace to our students. It means prioritizing joy, embracing moments of peace, and seeking support when we need it.

When we take care of ourselves, we set an example for our students. We show them that it is okay to prioritize mental health, that it is important to practice self-compassion, and that growth is a lifelong process. We teach them that strength is not about pushing through exhaustion but about knowing when to pause, reflect, and heal.

So let's commit to doing the work, not just the work of teaching, mentoring, and guiding, but the work of taking care of ourselves. Let's make space for rest. Let's embrace the idea that we, too, deserve the same kindness, patience, and care that we give so freely to others. Because when we are whole, when we are well, when we are thriving, we can create the kind of classrooms, schools, and communities where healing and growth are not just possible but inevitable.

Reflection Questions:

1. Katie starts out this chapter describing how many principals she's worked for. Discuss how many districts, classrooms, and buildings you've worked in.
2. With your group book study, discuss ways in which violence should be handled with parents and kids.
3. Drake represents many of our kids on a daily basis. Talk about a time you had to step up and love a kid into a success story.

4. Look at Stacy's list. How can you incorporate her methods into your classroom or school?
5. How do we change hearts and minds with this idea that grace must come before grades and people must come before data?
6. Tech addiction is real; how can we combat it and teach our students humanity?
7. Chris is an expert in Gen Z and Gen Alpha culture, and that is who we are teaching. Think about how our kids today are different from when we grew up.
8. Remember that rest is a requirement, not a reward. How do you rejuvenate your body, mind, heart, soul?

Chapter Seven Notes:

_____
_____
_____
_____
_____
_____
_____
_____
_____
_____
_____
_____

CHAPTER EIGHT

Building a Culture
of Community

Setting out to develop a book focusing on culture first in classrooms has been a very interesting endeavor. There are so many different elements that go into building that culture first classroom, and often, talking about one element leads into the next. Here, we want to talk about community. This, in and of itself, is complicated because community can have so many different meanings. For the sake of this chapter, we won't narrow the scope but rather let you follow the lead of the contributors and their interpretation of the term.

I grew up as a child of the 80s and 90s, which led to my love of the great sitcoms and movies of those decades. Television shows like *Cheers* and *Friends* bring up fond memories of my high school and college years. Likewise, movies such as *St. Elmo's Fire* remain close to my heart. What made shows like these so great was the connection and relationships the characters had with each other. Who can ever forget George Wendt walking into the bar saying, "Afternoon, everybody," with a rousing response of "NORM!" from the patrons at Cheers? In a word, community. We are drawn to these programs because the characters are all part of a collective group, a community. Ultimately, we all want to be part of a community and we should be working to create spaces in our classrooms where our students feel that same way.

As a teacher, especially when I was teaching middle school, I wanted to do everything I could to ensure every kid felt safe and welcome in my room. For that matter, I wanted them to see themselves on my walls and in my lessons. Like many teachers, I gathered information at the start of each school year to learn about their interests then would set out to find ways to incorporate them in my classroom lessons. One year in particular, I had several students who told me they really loved riding roller coasters. As luck would have it for these students, we had our physics unit early in the year, which meant I could get creative with types of motion and force. We researched the best rollercoasters in the country, watching several videos that shared the construction and science behind how they worked. One final element came from a teacher conference I attended, where I learned how to get students building their own roller coasters using pipe insulation tubes, tape, cardboard paper towel tubes, and marbles. The best part of this was how my students worked together, encouraged each other, and even celebrated the work of their peers. It was a great way to build community in my classroom.

Getting our students to a place where they feel the classroom is their space takes work and being very intentional. One excellent example of how this comes together can be found here with Tiffany Dorris. Read on and see how Tiffany builds community in her classroom.

One of the most exceptional and innovative educators I've had the privilege of working with is Ms. Tiffany Dorris. With years of

experience in the teaching profession, she continues to create meaningful and impactful experiences for her students. A two-time Teacher of the Year award winner, Tiffany would never boast about her own expertise, so it is with great pride that I sing her praises. She exemplifies grace, empathy, and a profound love for children that is truly unmatched by her peers. It's my pleasure to introduce you to the words of the incredible Tiffany Dorris.

CREATING SAFE CLASSROOMS THAT INCLUDE HIGH LEVELS OF LEARNING
Tiffany Dorris
Long Time Educator, Two-Time teacher of the Year, Middle School English Language Arts

"Building relationships with students is the single most important and impactful part of

> *my teaching career. I truly believe that students, especially middle schoolers, long to be seen, heard, and known; we all do. Content must always come after the powerful work of relationship building"*
> *~Tiffany Dorris*

Of course, this effort is a daily practice. Our good intentions don't cut it; we have to work daily on this. Daily practices for me include assigned seats, saying every student's name everyday, using "we" instead of "you" in correction ("We don't do that in our classroom." "We treat each other with respect." etc.). Cutdowns and hurtful jokes are nipped in the bud without making the classroom a place where no fun and laughter can happen. (Not always the easiest!) Finding the BEST in kids even when you have to stretch to do it. Tone and responses that are level and rarely emotional. Procedures that serve the classroom culture well. Also, the element of surprise goes a long way towards keeping kids engaged. How boring and counterproductive is it to have every day the same as the one before?

Creating a Positive School Culture
I am a forever learner in the teaching game, and I have learned so much from Brené Brown. She

says, "Culture eats strategy for breakfast," and I couldn't agree more. A positive school culture starts at the TOP: administrators who aren't afraid to confront issues at the root rather than passive-aggressively addressing the entire staff. Teachers who want to be there and want to do what is best for students. A positive school culture includes finding ways to celebrate and encourage one another, a place where risk-taking and creativity are encouraged rather than squashed. Brené also says, "Courage is contagious. When we choose courage, we make everyone around us a little better and the world a little braver." This is so true in our schools and classrooms!

Action Steps:

1. Don't just have good intentions; do the work to create a safe environment.
2. Don't allow meanness from students directed toward other students. Model kindness.
3. Create a space where kids can take big risks.

Developing a classroom community is not a one and done type of endeavor. This work is ever evolving and requires that we, as classroom leaders, are very intentional with the steps we take, the words we use, and even the activities we decide on for our students. An example from my time as a building principal would be in Bradlee Skinner's classroom. Bradlee had students who were learning how to leverage the power of social media, reaching out during class (yes, that's right, Bradlee let them use social media in class) and finding potential guest speakers for their speech class. At one point, his students had connected with and then hosted (via zoom) Taylor Mali, author of *What a Teacher Makes*. This only happens when the classroom is a community where everyone is included.

Another strong element that can often be overlooked in building the classroom community is the art of being intentional. Just like in an earlier exercise from Lindsay Titus (Chapter 5), being clear about what we want to see is best followed by being very intentional with the actions we take in the classroom to create that culture. Knowing from the beginning how you will share your expectations of mutual respect and understanding is critical. Being intentional about teaching students how you expect them to behave, interact, and communicate makes a tremendous difference. Teachers should begin each year by intentionally teaching the behaviors, interactions, and procedures they want to see from students. Then, from time to time, reteach those expectations. We can't simply assume that sharing it one time will get it to stick; we have to continue to teach and reteach our expectations if we are going to create the culture and the community we want in the classroom.

I once had a teacher on my campus during my principalship who told me she wasn't paid to teach kids how to behave. Not surprisingly, she had some of the biggest behavior issues in our school. It was during a pretty strong conversation (some might call it a disagreement) when I told her she needed to rethink that stance that she finally understood what I meant by intentionally teaching expectations in the classroom. Reluctantly, she agreed to spend a few minutes at the start of each class period sharing her expectations, being explicit on how it should look, and even sharing how students could expect her to respond and lead in the classroom. What a difference it made in her room. Discipline referrals went down and she even seemed happier at work.

At Harold Winkler Middle School, David James leads a wonderful staff of teachers who are very intentional with their efforts in building classroom culture and community. David and the rest of the staff utilize PLC time, along with their weekly Wolfpack Workshop voluntary Friday PD time to share best practices with each other around pedagogy, relationship building, and classroom culture.

We both have been connected to David James for a few years through his work with North Carolina's Middle Level Conference. Everyone should attend; he makes sure it is one of

the best middle school conferences in the nation. His love for his students jumps off the page, and when you meet him in person, you know he is the real deal. Enjoy Mr. James's words!

CLASSROOM CULTURE IS NOT ONLY FOR THE CLASSROOM
David James
Educator, North Carolina

"Be the teacher kids are talking about around the dinner table. The teacher and classroom kids are running back to the next day."
~Thomas Murray

Every year, we set off on a grand adventure with students to learn and grow together. As teachers, we start in August, influencing minds with our course content in hopes that something may stick as we move forward. The great teachers know that the course content is a vehicle for the more important work of influencing the hearts and behaviors of our students. We want them to be excited and passionate. We want them to learn empathy and understanding. We want them to be inquirers, deep thinkers, collaborators, and always persevere. The classroom serves as the environment where we undoubtedly will experience the hills and valleys of this journey. The intentional steps we take to create the structure, processes, and routines of this environment plays the most important role in how this adventure unfolds.

Each April, the seventh grade students at Harold E. Winkler Middle School in Concord, NC go on another grand adventure to Charleston, SC for an overnight field trip. If you have been on one of these trips as a teacher chaperone, you know they usually turn out to be an enjoyable and rewarding experience yet are incredibly exhausting and overwhelming at times. I have witnessed meltdowns from kids and adults, broken down buses, lost and stolen money, sickness, closed attractions without notice, and everything in between. Going on an overnight field trip with more than 250 twelve to fourteen year olds is not for the faint of heart and should 100 percent come with an added stipend and health insurance. That being said, the trip is always the highlight for students during their seventh grade school year, and that's why the seventh grade teaching group will always make it happen.

As the lead teacher on the lead bus, I get the same question from the tour guides and bus drivers from our trusted tour company each year. A question that I know is coming, but always brings a smile to my face, a tear to my eye, and a sense of pride in my heart, "These are the best kids we have ever been on a trip with. How do you do it?"

First, these heaven-sent individuals are usually retired teachers themselves that not only put 30+ years into a school building, but are using their retirement time to travel with over 250 young adolescents. They are incredibly patient, understanding of the kids' and adults' needs, and no matter what, will bend over backward to make the trip a positive experience. They have also seen it all. From puking and fighting to the bus breaking down and overstimulated adults on the verge of losing their minds and everything in between.

With this question, they are certainly providing a compliment to myself and the rest of the adults for how we positively communicate with each one of our kids by speaking to them in a tone of respect and empathy. These micro-interactions play a significant role in the overall enjoyment of the trip and the individuals on the outside' recognize that impact. In response, they are witnessing the students behave in a manner that has made their job more enjoyable while unquestionably bringing pride and, let's be honest, a bit of relief to myself as well.

But the question posed is not answered in the simplest terms that these individuals are more than likely looking for. It's not a secret, but it's also not a simple process. If there was a canned solution or program, we would all find success and be willing to travel overnight with kids to extend their learning outside of the classroom. Yet, I know many adults that are not willing to do this extra work, solely because of the fear of issues with student misconduct.

To get students to behave outside of our four walls we often bribe them with positive reinforcement, threaten to call their parents to pick them up four hours away if they misbehave, or we just hope they are not wearing the name of your school across their chest as they throw a piece of trash on the ground or yell and scream through the museum. Hope is a good place to start, but it's not a management strategy, and it certainly can't build classroom culture. So why, year after year, do we find success in and out of classroom experiences where students grow both academically and socially, free of student misbehavior and misconduct?

I am always proud to answer this question because it not only provides an opportunity to compliment the kids but also shines an important light on classroom culture. They are always taken aback when I respond to this question with, "It's not an accident."

The truth is, setting the culture in your classroom, your grade level hallway, and in your school starts on day one of your adventure and permeates everything you do as a community until day 180. If your daily interactions with kids are of respect, honesty, and forgiveness, they will treat others with respect, honesty, and forgiveness. If your classroom management includes consistency, communication, understanding, and empathy, those pillars of simply being a good person will also show up on a tour bus, in a restaurant, on the USS Yorktown Battleship, on the ferry ride to Fort Sumter, in the South Carolina Aquarium, and most importantly, during the overnight stay in a public hotel where middle school students are staying four to a room, without their parents for possibly the first time in their young lives.

It is not an accident when students make the correct choices. As the leaders of our classrooms, we have the biggest influence on the hearts, minds, and behaviors of our students daily. A strong classroom culture starts on day one with agreed classroom expectations, and they don't stop when you leave the school building. Witness as your students carry these understandings to the auditorium for the end of year awards celebration, to the gymnasium for a whole-school pep rally, during strict end of year testing environments, and away from the school building for academic field trips. Marvel in the compliments from others due to the behavior of your students and know that your processes and structures made them successful and it was, in fact, not an accident.

Have you got this mastered? Take it a step further by collaborating with your grade level colleagues to establish hallway expectations not only for students, but also adults. How are we welcoming students into the hallway each day? What are the agreed upon Homeroom expectations for the entire grade level? How are we positively communicating to kids without ridicule and sarcasm? How are students entering and leaving each classroom? What should students do to use the restroom, visit the school counselor, or leave the classroom in general? What is the process for students who are late to class? What are the expectations for students when entering the cafeteria, cleaning up their lunch, and heading back to class? How do we walk in the hallway so as not to disrupt the learning process of our classmates? Take the time to have these conversations as a professional learning community. Be a leader in guiding these conversations and communicating the importance of consistency as the teacher-leaders in the hallway.

Establish the culture you want with your group of students through intentional decision making. Be proud of the work you have done and celebrate the achievements of your staff and students in the small moments of compliance and following expectations. Take them on an overnight field trip. You will be amazed at the influence you have made on their lives based on the compliments you receive from those around your group. Enjoy the adventure, and don't settle on mediocrity. Your successful classroom culture will carry you and your students past the classroom walls.

Action Steps:

1. Be like David, and have your course content be the vehicle to the more important work of influencing hearts and minds.
2. If able, try to take your students on an adventure, like David and his colleagues do for their seventh graders.
3. Work together as a team to help mold children into their best versions.

Community can be so much more than just what happens inside our classroom. I have been in many buildings where staff are working to make sure the students inside the walls feel represented in their school. As a principal, my staff created murals in the building to help tell our story to visitors. As well, one mural was a set of silhouettes designed to represent who our students were when they were *not* on campus.

Many communities have a great deal of ethnic diversity, with students coming from many different countries and wide backgrounds. Working to ensure all students, regardless of their heritage, feel welcome and included in the community takes great focus. A great example here is the work found in Andrea Bitner's school community.

We had the pleasure of connecting with Andrea at different conferences throughout the years. She is insightful when it comes to leading and teaching our English Language Learners. Full of wisdom, real stories, and a true love of helping kids launch into learning, it is a blessing to bring you Andrea's words.

WE ARE NOT A HOLDING PLACE: WE ARE A LAUNCHING PAD
Andrea Bitner
EL Teacher, Author, Speaker

"Our English Language Learners and families aren't looking for customers; they are looking for investors. Learning English takes time. Mastering how to confidently reach

and teach our ELs takes time. Their opportunity for a free education with us is limited. I'm here on their behalf. Education is opportunity; education is freedom. What's your P.LA.N.? Be Proud, Be Loud, Be Ambitious, Never Give Up."
~Andrea Bitner

How do your hallways say hello, goodbye, please stay, and don't give up today? The average school building has hundreds, if not thousands, of young people who stroll, trek, wander, patrol, and oftentimes, leap or run through it for at least 2,250 minutes per week. These halls and walls serve as their primary home for over a decade of their lives.

Do your students see these hallways as their home away from home? Do they see this academic, social, and emotional center for learning as a celebration of the past, a recognition of the present, and a bridge to their future? In other words, is your building seen as an extension of your community, or as a cliff that kids jump off of each morning? And if they weren't required to show up each day, would they still attend your school?

ReLita Clarke says, "If I can see it, I can be it." Today, I encourage you to begin an audit of the halls and walls of your school. Who and what do your students and families SEE when they step into your space? And more importantly, have you incorporated, celebrated, and not just tolerated, their vision of what they want to BE?

In our school district, we represent over 500 English Language Learners with 31 different languages. The first thing my principal did in his inaugural year in leadership was to place floor to ceiling length flags with labels from all of their countries in the main hallways of our building. As the students and their families entered our school, they were bubbling with validation, conversation, and excitement.

"Ms. B!" they cried. "Did you SEE Pakistan's flag? Did you see Guatemala's flag? Did you see the US flag? I took a picture for my Mom!"
Another parent approached me with her Say Hi app that she used for translation. She had recently arrived from the Ukraine and was appreciative of the recognition and connection. "Дуже дякую!" (Thank you so much!) she said. Мені це подобається!" (I love this!) This was our first step in letting our students and families know: We see you.

The next step is to connect our kids within these halls and walls to our local community as they travel through their journey of figuring out who they want to be. In my 24 years of serving in this field with K-12 students who hold a variety of school labels, here is what I know for sure, every student and family, no matter what they want to be, are looking for the same three things: to be respected, to feel accepted, and to be admired. To accomplish this, we create our school as a community bridge, we host family engagement nights throughout the school year that include the four Fs: family, food, fun, and free.

It is during these events that we are intentional about connecting families with each other who speak the same languages. We also invite alumni EL students to return each year and speak to our high school kids about their experiences and encourage them to sustain their positive attitudes and work ethic as well as learn from the successes and mistakes of those who sat in the very same chairs. We connect our students to support teachers, office staff, maintenance teams, cafeteria squads, coaches, band directors, club leaders, and anyone we can find in the entire district who can serve as a role model for our kids. This *we* before *me* mentality (thanks, Jon Gordon!) has served us with plate upon plate of successful supports for our students and families to lean into.

We also look at the roof of our building not as a holding place but as a launching pad. Our students leave the building often; they travel to connect with EL students in other local districts. They attend vocational schools, technical schools, high school college programs, conferences, work release allowances, internships, and community volunteer organizations. Our students take field trips with all our ELs districtwide to expand their knowledge and connection of students who they can identify with and be role models for. These experiences catapult their awareness of future opportunities, vindicate how their in-school skills can be authentically applied, and prompt them to remember why they are celebrated and not just tolerated inside and outside of the halls and walls of our school AND community.

Our hallways say hello, goodbye, please stay, and don't give up today. Our kids know that they can always share with us what they want to be, because we are dedicated to helping them see that our school is an extension of our community. They are the future global leaders of the world, and we are honored to have had the opportunity to lead them, dig down into the weeds with them, and succeed with them throughout this chapter of their lives.

Action Steps:

1. Think about your classroom; does it embody, "If I can see it, I can be it?"
2. Incorporate family and community nights at your school.
3. Celebrate all students from all cultures.

The term community can represent so many different groups. Sometimes, we think of our community as what is happening inside our walls, but in this next section we focus on the community at large. Schools are naturally a part of their community, but not every community member knows what is happening in the school or maybe even feels welcome to be a part of the school.

First impressions are most likely the way people will remember our schools and our classrooms. As a building leader, I was very intentional about that and made sure our building secretaries had a positive way of answering the phone and greeting parents, vendors, and other guests to our school. That impression might be the reason they say something great about your school or perhaps something not so great.

I first met Joy when I did some work in her district in 2021. She is the kind of principal the people love. She is visible, joyful, and unfailingly kind. She continues to be a beacon of light for her staff, so read her words on first impressions because they matter!

FIRST IMPRESSIONS
Joy Osborne
Assistant Principal

"Community is the heartbeat that keeps the building alive."
~Joy Osborne

A must when it comes to establishing an amazing school culture is setting a good first impression the minute someone walks through the door and is greeted with a smile from the office staff. Student work is seen in the hallways to promote achievement and represent a sense of belonging and extreme pride in the work our students accomplish. Celebrations are heard around the school, and relationships are evident by the mutual respect between staff and students.

Community must be the heartbeat that keeps the building alive.

Action Steps:

1. What does the community see when they first walk in? Does something need to change?
2. Put out student work in the hallway, like Joy.
3. Celebrate your students loud and proud!

The term community can apply to so many different things. The goal in this chapter was to focus on a few of its meanings and to share some insights into how best to leverage and lean into community. There are a few very common themes that come up in each of the passages and throughout the chapter.

First, being intentional about sharing what you are expecting and really teaching those expectations goes a long way in achieving your goals. Second, there is an element of understanding and acceptance that is inherent in good school communities. We should be focusing on who the people are who are part of the community, be very clear in how we want them to participate in our community, work to help them feel included and to see themselves as valuable members of the community, then celebrate the members of our community.

Reflection Questions:

1. How are you currently creating a culture of high expectations?
2. What steps do you have in place in your classroom to intentionally teach expectations, similar to David James?
3. Andrea talks about her school displaying flags for every country represented in their population. What are some ways that students are seeing their culture and/or heritage embraced in your classroom or school?
4. Walk your entrance way and hallways as if you are a visitor. What do you notice about the first impressions your school makes for visitors? What might you do in your school or your classroom to capitalize on the opportunity to make a positive impression for visitors?

Chapter Eight Notes:

_____

_____

_____

_____

CHAPTER NINE

Accountability, Growth, and Legacy

When Darrin and I first started discussing our book we kept saying, classroom management. "This will be a book that helps teachers with classroom management," but as we began to craft it and inviting the best in the business to contribute, we quickly learned it was much more than management, but in actuality, as the one-and-only Kim Campbell says, "If you can't manage them, you can't teach them." And if you can't teach them, they won't learn. The result? A quick and steady descent into chaos, and once that door opens, it breeds disrespect, disrupts learning, and, most importantly, puts the safety and well-being of everyone at risk. That's not just an inconvenience; it's a crisis, so please indulge me as I share what I believe is a simple yet best practice when it comes to creating the type of classroom environment where students thrive.

What is the key to creating a well-managed, structured, and engaging classroom, one where students feel safe, valued, and ready to learn? It starts with setting clear expectations and holding everyone – including yourself – accountable.

First, **learn their names.** And not just that, be relentless about pronouncing them correctly. Your students will notice if you make the effort, and that effort tells them, "I see you. You matter." On day one, skip calling out names from the attendance list – your students aren't loyal to you yet, but they are loyal to each other. If you mispronounce a name in front of the entire class, they will save face with their peers before they show respect to you, and that can be a core, negative memory for them. Instead, as students work on a simple assignment, take the time to go around the room, greet them individually, and ask how they pronounce their names and what they prefer to go by. That small moment of connection sets the tone for everything that follows.

From that first day, **address issues immediately**. This is not about being harsh; it's about setting expectations with warmth and consistency. Use the *Love and Logic* approach, gentle but firm. If a student talks out of turn, instead of snapping, smile and say, "Oh, goodness, we don't talk out of turn in this class. Do you have a question?" Then, rinse and repeat. As my good friend P. Sloan Joseph says, "What you don't address will become a mess!" And that, my friends, is the absolute truth.

Procedures. Procedures. **Procedures.** How do students ask for a pencil? What's the process for using the restroom? How do they ask a question? Every single routine must be taught, modeled, and reinforced. Don't assume they just *know* how to do things the way you want them done – teach them. Create a culture where your classroom runs like a well-oiled machine, where expectations are clear and consistent. If you need ideas, reach out, I have an entire set of classroom procedures complete with a fun group quiz to reinforce them.

And we've discussed the elephant in the room **- phones.** Ban them. Students don't need them. Almost every district post-COVID is one-to-one, meaning students already have Chromebooks, iPads, or other devices for educational use.

Phones don't belong in the learning environment. They are distractions, and the moment you allow them in sight, you're competing with social media, texts, and notifications for your students' attention. Take control. Make it a required procedure that phones are put away, not as a punishment, but as a classroom norm.

Speaking of devices, establish **clear procedures for technology use.** If a student misuses their school-issued device, what happens next? Is there a warning system? A call home? A temporary loss of privileges? Whatever the consequences are, make sure they are clearly defined and consistently enforced across your team. A unified approach prevents arguments and creates structure.

Let's talk about **music in the classroom.** Many students will insist they learn better while listening to their own music with lyrics, but brain research says otherwise. Studies show that listening to music with lyrics while working can lower their IQ by ten points. That's an entire letter grade. Instead, if you want music in the background, choose instrumental soundtracks, classical music, or lo-fi beats to boost focus without distraction.

Group work should be structured and purposeful**.** Establish roles that allow every student to contribute in a way that plays to their strengths. Maybe one is the Leader, another the Scribe, a third the Researcher, a fourth the Runner, and a fifth the Speaker. And enforce the No Cross-Pod Talking rule. Students should be engaged with their group, not shouting across the room to their best friend. The more structured the group work, the more productive, and enjoyable it becomes.

At the heart of all of this is **relevance and engagement.** If you want students to behave, if you want them to be invested, your lessons need to matter to them. "Because we've always done it this way" is not a reason to keep doing anything. Look at your standards, look at your students, and ask yourself: How can I make this meaningful? If students see value in what they're learning, they're less likely to act out and more likely to engage.

And don't forget, **revisit expectations after every long break.** The reset button exists for a reason. Students need reminders, and you need to re-establish the tone of your classroom after time away.

Most importantly, **have fun with your students.** Laugh with them. Enjoy them. Build relationships that go beyond academics. When students respect you, when they feel safe, when they know they are part of something bigger than themselves, that's when the magic happens. Classroom management isn't about control; it's about creating an environment where everyone - students and teachers alike - can thrive.

This work is hard. But it's also worth it. Every day, you are shaping experiences, guiding young minds, and creating memories that will last a lifetime. *What you do matters.* So, do it with purpose, do it with joy, and do it well; our kids deserve it!

I taught across the building from Kristin Linholm for two years. She is kind and hilarious. She is the teacher you want for your own kids. She keeps high expectations in her room while maintaining fun and a love of learning. Take her words on teaching, and put them into practice for yourself because this advice comes from an exceptional and award-winning teacher.

LEAVE YOUR CAMPGROUND BETTER THAN YOU FOUND IT
Kristin Linholm, M.Ed.
District Teacher of the Year, Sixth Grade Teacher

"In all that you do in your classroom, strive each day to delight, inform, and inspire."
~Kristin Linholm

"Leave your campground better than you found it," is an old Boy Scout motto that was said to my siblings and me by our dad when we were growing up. This statement resonated with me even more when I became a teacher and had my own classroom. My mindset every year is, *How can each child leave my classroom at the end of the year being better in some way than they were when I met them on the first day of school?* Focusing on the bigger picture gives me clear goals on how to approach establishing community in my classroom each year.

Everyone wants to feel like they are a part of something, and this desire becomes vital in the classroom. Rules and expectations, rules and expectations, rinse and repeat. Put in the time teaching these at the first of the year; it will be worth it. Why do I spend so much time working on my classroom expectations? Because I've learned:

- Kids feel safe when they know what is expected of them.
- Kids feel safe when they know their teacher is going to be consistent.

- Kids feel safe when they know who is driving the boat.

My rules aren't just the typical rules for a secure, physical space either. I present a whole lesson on manners and how to speak to others. I'm a big fan of politeness and respectfulness. Once we all know how we will be treating each other, my classroom becomes a comfortable space to speak, give opinions, discuss, try, make mistakes, advocate, and grow.

Here are a few of my musts when it comes to my classroom and a positive school culture:

- **Make your classroom space a place YOU want to be.** You will spend more time in your room than in your home at some points in the year. Spend some time before school decorating your room so you are proud of your space and want to be there. If your room brings you joy, it will bring the kids joy too.
- **Establish connections with other teachers.** Whether within your grade level, content area, or team, create community with the other teachers. If no one is getting teachers together or aiding in building staff connections, be that person at your school. Celebrate each other. Kids like seeing that their teachers are also friends. As I am

writing this, I can hear teachers in the hallway laughing; it matters.

- **Be a part of your school community.** Go to the band concerts, the sporting events, and the vocal music performances. Dress up when there is a Dress Up Day. Show up and support your students.

- **Follow the school rules too.** School/district rules need to be followed in the classroom. For example, if there is a no phone policy and you feel like that isn't important to you in your room, be a team player and follow the school rule anyway. When one member of the staff doesn't follow through with the school rules, it carries over to the other classrooms and affects the school and staff climate.

- **When you make a mistake or are wrong, admit it.** This seems like an odd suggestion, but admitting when you are wrong about something makes it okay for kids to make mistakes too.

- **Get to know your students.** Always try to learn new information about your kids. Know their names! Ask them questions about themselves. Some students, especially in middle school, try really hard to be invisible, but see them, and try to learn more about them. Bethany Hill says, "Every child you pass in the hall has a story that needs to be heard. Maybe you are the one meant to hear it."

- **Show grace.** We all have those days where we would like to yell, "Do over!" When a student chooses to say or do something that is negative, we will absolutely have a conversation. However, I always like to talk to that student the next day and remind them that it's a new day, and we are starting fresh.

It takes some time to teach all the rules and procedures for your classroom at the beginning of the year, but it is worth the effort. When my first-of-the-year boot camp is finished, Linholmland is ready for a year full of wonderful!

Action Steps:

1. Is your classroom a place where all students belong?
2. Reach out to a teacher you don't really know, and get to know them.
3. Apologize to kids when it is necessary.

Tennessee Williams once said, "All cruel people describe themselves as paragons of frankness." We've seen it; we've heard it. "I just tell it like it is; that is just who I am. Sorry if you are offended. I have boundaries." Well, I'm going to wholeheartedly push back on this statement made by many adults worldwide. A dog-eat-dog world shouldn't exist. You can have boundaries and still lean into compassion. We can disagree and have conflict in a kind manner, and we need to actively teach our children to do the same.

As a teacher of kids between the ages of 11-15, I've seen firsthand the effects that the pandemic, tech addiction issues, and social isolation has had on our kids. They come to us without the ability to have a healthy conversation or to participate in healthy discourse, and we must teach this skill. And it is not a one and done, check this standard off the list type of lesson. We must actively, relentlessly teach our children humanity everyday.

There are a lot of things as educators that we cannot change about our broken system. We have people making laws about what we do each day who have never taught a day in their lives. We have community members trying to mandate what we teach, how we teach it, and the list goes on. It is an odd thing we see in our profession; just because someone once sat in a classroom as a student, they think they know what it is like to walk in our shoes. It isn't like this in other professions. Just because you once went in for surgery on your knee does not make you qualified to start up your own orthopedic clinic and begin doling out new ACLs and MCLs to the general population. It seems silly to even say that, but for some reason, in our profession, this is exactly what happens, but we can't hyper focus on things we can't control. What we can control is our classrooms, our four walls, and teaching our kids how to be good and decent human beings.

Kindness reigns supreme in my English class. We can't get to the innovation and life-changing lessons unless we have a classroom where we are valuing and celebrating each and every one of us. Because when we teach kindness, humanity, and integrity, belonging comes next, and when our students feel true belonging in our spaces, that is when we literally help save the lives of our deeply lonely students who need a place to belong and be safe. How do I do it? We practice, we practice again, and we practice some more. We partake in Socratic Seminars using literature that represents my students; we learn the correct way to have discourse in a kind manner, and work collaboratively using each other's strengths. We allow vulnerability to be a superpower in my space.

At the beginning of the school year, I feel a lesson that is crucial is my annual, "Spread The Word To End The Word" lesson. I begin class with instrumental music while my students walk in and read the board. It says, "Write about someone you know who lives with a disability." I share about my daughter who lives with a profound visual impairment. I share about my best friend's son who lives with Down Syndrome, and that when she hears the R-word, she cries and it causes her great pain. Most of the time, my students just need education on why this is a hurtful word. I share with them a video from ESPN called, *One Love* based on NFL star Joe Haden's brother, Jacob, who lives with a cognitive disability. Joe Haden will school anyone who says the R-word in front of him. He says, "Buy a dictionary!" This powerful man of character and courage breaks down in tears over his love for his brother Jacob. This gives my students permission to be vulnerable as well and they begin to open up about people in their lives that happen to live with a disability. This begins our journey to belonging, our journey to life-changing lessons, and our journey to learn how to be empathetic by learning the stories of others.

As adults, we get the opportunity to choose kindness over frustration, and kindness over anger, and kindness over cruelty. The next time you hear, "Well, that is just how I am; I just tell it like it is!" I implore you to push back, and show our kids that kindness reigns supreme and that you can stand by your values whilst also being relentlessly kind to others.

Coach Sara Mobley is the epitome of a trustworthy adult for kids. She wields great power as a coach and is an icon in the spaces in her school. I had the privilege of working alongside Sara in the trenches of our school. We were in a foxhole on a daily basis, and I wouldn't have wanted anyone else with me. She had my back, and she had the backs of the students entrusted to her each day. Enjoy the words of Coach Sara Mobley.

TEAM MENTALITY
Sara Mobley
PE and Health Coach

*"Teaching is a passion, and it's our job to spread that
light to our students!"
~Sara Mobley*

Classroom management is extremely important in my gym and health room. To have a high level of this, I must stay consistent with my rules and regulations. This establishes a routine for my kids, and they learn how to buy into our team culture. When the students believe they are a team and begin to move in the same direction, this keeps our classroom environment safe. My number one classroom philosophy is that everyone belongs. I teach the kids that no matter what level of life they are on, once they walk into my classroom, they are all welcome, and we function as a team. This also cuts down on bullying in my classroom and causes students to learn to embrace everyone.

Action Steps:

1. Establish routines in specials too.
2. Foster a team mentality; everyone wants to belong.
3. Teach students to embrace differences.

Consistency is key, no question about it. It is quite a challenge for anyone to work in an environment where they just don't know what to expect from day to day. Developing those clear procedures and guidelines, as Sara points out, make it easy for students to come into the room and get down to learning. Reading Sara's passage made me think of a teacher I worked with who oversaw our pool, Wendy Bider. She taught PE/Swim several times per day. You can imagine how challenging having students, both male and female, changing into swimsuits, being in the water, and then changing back can be. This could be a management nightmare. But just like Sara, Wendy had great focus on ensuring everyone felt welcome but also followed clear procedures. It was always a pleasure to spend time in her pool classroom.

Throughout this book I have talked about the importance of being intentional. In this next section, Pat Terry takes being intentional to a whole new level, and I love it.

Pat Terry is one of my absolute favorite people, not just as a teacher, but as a human being. He's hilarious, talented, and rocks a glorious beard. Beyond that, he is one of the most skilled middle school teachers in education today. His classroom is filled with Socratic seminars, project-based learning, and constant laughter. I wouldn't be the educator I am today without Coach Terry by my side for many years. I've learned so much from him, and I continue to do so. So, take in the wisdom of this master educator, and let it inspire you to grow.

BE INTENTIONAL
Patrick Terry
Award-Winning Social Studies Educator

"Educators: it seems as if there are a million things to do, but FOCUS on what is best for your students. All the other stuff will come in time."
~Pat Terry

I wish I had some amazing activity that makes all students listen to you or an icebreaker that makes you the favorite teacher in the building for the rest of the year, but I don't. What I do have is something that drives my practice as a middle school social studies teacher: BE INTENTIONAL. If the phrase was a little catchier I would start making t-shirts of it that you could buy online next to a sign that says "Eat, Pray, Love."

What I mean by intentional is to plan out moments that students will remember. I like to use humor as a way to build relationships with students, so I set up a time of the day to do just that. You know that awkward time after clean-up and before the bell rings, that is the time we tell the Joke of the Day. I start by telling students really bad dad jokes, and they love it. They start bringing their own jokes to class and it begins to take on a life of its own. On days I forget or don't have a joke handy, students remind me, "What about the joke of the day Mr. Terry?"

These little breaks in class are the thing that most students remember long after they leave middle school.

I am also intentional about where I set up my desk in my classroom. I have two desks, my normal desk with trays and my very long To-Do list and another stand up desk, more like a broken down podium that I pieced back together and found in the desk graveyard or the furniture discard room at my school. Every school has one; I implore you to go treasure hunting in yours. I use the stand up desk when students are in class, from there, I can take attendance, answer emails, run the presentation on the smart board while being present with my class. Make sure to set your room up for the best range of movement for kids and yourself. Create lanes for you to be able to walk around your room with ease and talk to each student. When students are working individually or with their groups, take laps around your classroom, ask them if they need help, give praise when you hear something great or feedback if something needs to be corrected. Sitting at your desk or staying at the front of your room only creates a barrier between you and your students. Get those steps in!

My last bit of advice on intentionality, is around inevitable conflict with a student because it will happen, and that is okay. Our students are learning not only academically, but also socially and emotionally. At the beginning of the school year, I explain my classroom management plan to my students. The first time I correct a student, it is a warning. Just a simple, "Hey, Jimmy, please stop playing the drums with your pencils; it is distracting others." But if little Jimmy continues to live out his fantasy as the lead drummer for Led Zeppelin, I say to him, "Jimmy, please step into the hall." I am not angry. I am not yelling. I am simply inviting Jimmy to the hallway for a chat. If he resists, I stand by the door and continue to invite him while keeping my voice and body language calm.

When I meet him in the hallway, I have a script that I follow. My first question is, "What are we going to talk about?" or "Why are we in the hallway?" I usually get a generic but honest response like, " I was being a distraction" or "I dunno, I was being loud, I guess." From there, I explain what happened from my point of view and ask the student what needs to be changed to help them be successful when they come back into class. Sometimes, kids are just jittery and need to move. PERFECT; go get a drink of water and come back to class. Or my seating chart missed the fact that I unknowingly sat two best friends next to each other, and they couldn't stop talking. Other times, it can be something more serious like problems at home or at school.

After the conversation is over, I make sure to explain to them the next step, and it usually goes, "Okay, thank you for helping me solve this problem. I do NOT plan on calling home or telling a principal about this. You are NOT in trouble, but if the problem continues, consequences may come. Now, let's get back to class." My point is that I am intentional about how I deal with conflict and, I never want to set myself or my students up for a lose-lose situation with me and a student arguing in front of the class because the student will do more to save face in front of their peers than they will to listen to their teacher. Give them an option.

Being intentional doesn't only apply to what I rambled on about, it can apply to all parts of your classroom ecosystem. A well placed meme can get you really far in a boring lesson or make some time to share good things going on in your students' lives. Unstructured time is okay as long as you have a plan for it. So, go out there and get that t-shirt made; be intentional!

Action Steps:
1. Be intentional about building a fun culture in your room.
2. Think about the placement of your desk and how you can better serve the kids in your care.
3. Think about how you can emulate Mr. Terry's joke of the day, or how he squashes any disrespect in his room.

Pat and I taught on the same team for years before our careers took us in different directions – me stepping into the role of an Instructional Coach and him following his boss, his Air Force wife, across the world to teach while taking care of their two boys. When he packed up and moved overseas, I felt the loss immediately. He wasn't just a colleague; he was a friend, a partner in educational mischief, and someone who made the daily grind of teaching both fun and fulfilling. But no matter the miles between us, we've stayed in touch, sharing stories, ideas, and the occasional classroom battle strategy.

His journey has been an adventure – teaching in Japan, returning stateside, jumping into a local district, then preparing to move yet again. That military life is no joke, but he embraces it fully, and I have no doubt that wherever he goes, he brings that same passion for teaching and engagement that made our time together so memorable.

When I set out to write this book about classroom management, culture, and engagement, there was no way I could do it without having my buddy Pat contribute. His insights, humor, and experiences were too valuable not to include.

We hopped on the phone multiple times during the planning phase, and each call quickly spiraled into fits of laughter as we reminisced about our time at our old school. Those weren't just classrooms we taught in; they were stages for storytelling, places of controlled chaos, and incubators for creativity. I still remember teaching Greek Mythology with my staff of education power, pacing around the room, weaving stories of Zeus and Hades like some kind of ancient bard. Meanwhile, Pat was next door, wielding an enormous ruler that practically stretched to the ceiling, bringing history to life with grand, sweeping gestures.

One day, just for fun, I sent a student into his classroom on a covert mission – to steal the ruler. Not one to be outdone, Pat sent a kid into my class to take my staff. And so, the great ransom war began. Students had to write poetic ransom notes, assigning ridiculous tasks for the other teacher to complete in order to retrieve their stolen teaching props. We had to write rhyming couplets, do jumping jacks, and even compete in a Math Olympics before our prized classroom tools were returned. The students were fully invested, negotiating trades and devising clever demands, all while completely immersed in learning – without even realizing it.

Then there was the day the power went out across the entire building. No electricity. No projectors. No computers. Just teachers, students, and an unexpected challenge. Instead of panicking or defaulting to busywork, Pat and I did what we did best - we improvised. We combined our classes in the brightest room we could find, pulled desks together, and set up a spontaneous debate tournament on educational topics. No scripts, no tech - just pure discussion, argumentation, and critical thinking. The students loved it. They were engaged, energized, and debating until the final bell rang. Years later, those same students still bring it up when they run into us. It wasn't just a lesson; it was an experience.

And that's the core of what we believe about teaching - it should be an experience. It should be engaging, it should be fun, and it should be filled with moments that stick with students long after they leave our classrooms. Whether it's staging an epic ransom battle over stolen teaching props, adjusting on the fly when the lights go out, or simply bringing passion and energy to every lesson, the best classrooms are the ones where learning feels alive.

Pat and I may not teach in the same building anymore, but the lessons we learned together about creativity, culture, and connection are ones I carry with me every single day. And if I can pass those lessons on to other educators, then this book is already a success.

It is interesting how we bond over similarities and are drawn to people who are like us. Brian Martin and I have both been basketball coaches, have a love of the NFL (him the Bills, me the Broncos), and share a podcasting space. But it is much more than that with Brian, he carries a philosophy and an outlook on life with infectious energy and optimism. He takes positive thinking to a whole other level. Brian Martin is one of the best human beings I have ever met. He truly is a teaching champion from his classroom to the court to his podcast.

MICRO MOMENTS
Brian Martin
Second Grade Teacher, Speaker,
Host of the *Teaching Champions* Podcast

One of the most impactful ways to build classroom culture is through the messaging you send to your students. From the moment you meet them at the doorway of the classroom, to the moment they leave for the day, and every moment in between, with every interaction you send a message. If you let those you serve know they belong, are valued, appreciated, and loved, the classroom culture you create will be next level.

Many people talk about the importance of starting each student's day with a positive greeting at the door. There are also people that talk about ending the day in a positive way. While both are important, it is not often emphasized how every micro interaction throughout the day is an opportunity to create a connection. Dr. John Gottman, one of the most influential relationship psychologists in the world, has discovered through his research that the strongest relationships have a "magic ratio" of five positives for every one negative interaction. Bringing this research into practice in the classroom may help us be conscious of the messages we are sending. People remember the negative far more than the positive; therefore, it is necessary for the positive to greatly outweigh the negative.

Theodore Roosevelt once said, "No one cares how much you know, until they know how much you care." If we desire strong connections with our students, we must be aware of the message we send to each of them. There are students with whom we easily and naturally meet the magic ratio. Then there are students with whom we miss the mark. It may be the students needing more redirection, the quiet ones, or the ones we do not instantly connect with. Be deliberate in your words and actions throughout the day. Go out of your way for small moments of connection. Make a point to connect with all the students in some way. Fill the spaces you are in and those you serve with intentional, deliberate, and affirming words of appreciation.

There may be a magic ratio; however, creating strong relationships is not magic at all. It happens one micro interaction at a time. Let students know they matter by how you celebrate them inside your classroom. Show interest in them and the things they enjoy. Let your actions show you respect who they are and that you see their gifts. Let them know through the notes you leave on their desks, emails and letters you send to their parents, and all the ways you choose to recognize them that they are valued. With first bumps and high fives, show students they are appreciated. Make it apparent, with your positive energy and enthusiasm, you are there to celebrate the successes, support the struggles, and cheer them on every step of the way.

It is not only the daily greetings or send-offs that build relationships. The micro interactions and messaging that lives in the middle is where the magic is found. All those moments and the intentionality behind them create amazing classroom culture.

Action Steps:

1. What message are you sending to students?
2. Create meaningful micro moments.
3. Greet kids at the door each and every day.

When I was a JV basketball coach, I worked under a fantastic head coach named Dave Vance. Dave taught me so much as a coach about accountability, planning, and being intentional with everything we did on the practice court so that it would translate into what we wanted to see on game day. Nearly all of those lessons are very applicable to how we build our Culture First Classroom.

Be prepared for everything. Our practice plans were structured down to the minute and were posted at the start of practice. Players knew before the practice began what they were doing and how we'd measure success. No surprises, just focused on details. **Compete.** Every day in practice we should be competing with each other so we get the best out of ourselves on game day. We used the scoreboard and game clock for every drill, every teaching session, even our breaks. Players should be able to lean into competition and push each other in all we do to bring out our best. **Never be surprised.** If you've done the work in practice it should translate to the game. You should never be surprised by how your team plays because you've put in the work, you were intentional with all your preparation, now trust them to do what they've practiced.

All of these are such great lessons in teaching. Dave wasn't just a great coach, he was a great teacher. I will wrap this section up with another thing I learned from Dave, specifically a phrase he used frequently. That's the BOTTOM LINE. Dave used this phrase with our team, and honestly with our coaching staff, to reinforce that when the ball went in the air, the bottom line was whether or not our players, or us as coaches, would perform at the level we expected and had been taught.

So, the bottom line here is this, as the leaders of your classroom you have to make the decision on what you expect and how you will reinforce those expectations. Accountability can be done in many ways but it is best done collectively. Developing the "leave your campground better than you found it" mentality in our classrooms is a great way to build shared accountability with our students. It also helps to grow pride in both the space and in their work; it sets a standard for what you expect and what you will accept. Create clear and strong routines that students know from memory to not only save time but also to continue building accountability with your students. Be intentional, as Pat Terry shared, about everything you do. And finally, look for those micro moments. You never know when one might create a huge impact in the life of a child.

Remember that each and every day you work with kids you are building your legacy. Writing this book has brought back so many memories and driven a lot of reflection for me on my time in the classroom as well as my time leading a building and a district. Every one of us is leaving a legacy. When you lean into the opportunity to build a culture first classroom, you understand you are leading in the classroom, not just teaching. You embrace that relationships matter and that focusing on who students are and what they need is a key to success. You know that it takes a community and loving accountability to grow our students into the amazing human beings they ultimately will become. That's the bottom line. Now, it's time to launch your *Culture First Classroom!*

Reflection Questions:

1. This chapter begins with Katie sharing the keys to accountability in the classroom. One of the areas Katie discussed that people miss on frequently is developing procedures. Reflect on the procedures you currently have

in the classroom. Which procedures are working really well for you? Are there some that need a boost?
2. Kristin Lindholm shares a few "musts" for her classroom as it pertains to positive school culture. Which of her musts resonated most with you? Is this something you could implement into your classroom or your routine?
3. Pat Terry talked about being intentional with everything you do in the classroom. Thinking more about his writing, what are some things you do intentionally that positively impact the culture of your classroom?
4. Are you ready to build *your* Culture First Classroom?

Chapter Nine Notes:

_____
_____
_____
_____
_____
_____
_____
_____
_____
_____
_____
_____
_____
_____
_____

CONCLUSION

*"Leadership is not about titles, positions, or flowcharts.
It is about one life influencing another."
~John C. Maxwell*

In my opinion, in this education journey, mission, and call on our lives, it is important to remember that not one of us is more essential than another, so titles be damned. And that sentiment goes for all adults in a school building, in a district ecosystem which is vital to the health and safety of the children entrusted to us. Your title doesn't matter; you are a leader in your school, and we must value each other as such because we need every last one of us each and every day. The superintendent is not more important than our head custodians, bus drivers, cafeteria workers, teachers, paraprofessionals and the list goes on. We all have the ability to alter the course of a child's life for the better and for this reason alone, we must link arms and hearts to help children on their path to success, and walk alongside them in moments of hardship.

If I know the school resource officer has a special connection with a certain kid that needs a bit more love and attention than I can give him in my room with thirty other children, it is a comfort to reach out to our resource officer for help. If I have more capacity to handle four or five extra students in my room on any given day because I have those types of tools in my tool belt, send them to me. If I know a student is crazy in love with band, and I know our band director can intervene with this certain kid when things go off the rails in English class, it is an honor to have the privilege of reaching out to this rockstar band director as a lifeline for certain students. If I know a student is hungry, and my snack drawer is empty, and I can call a cafeteria worker or two for help, it boosts not only my sense of safety and worth, but all of us.

We need each other, and our students depend on all of us having the courage to be able to lean on one another in times of need. This is how we band together and have the kind of culture we all crave, the kind of culture that people don't leave, the kind of culture in which we have applicant after applicant trying to work in our districts, in our schools. Educators have the power to change lives. Whether through a kind word, a moment of extra attention, or the courage it takes to hold students to high standards because that is doing what is relentlessly right for kids. Educators plant seeds of possibility that often flourish long after the school bell rings. But the ripple effect doesn't end with the students. When teachers uplift one child, they uplift families, communities, and even future generations.

Education is not without its challenges, and we know this. There are long hours, limited resources, and the emotional toll of investing deeply in students' lives. It is messy, human work, but we must prevail because the impact is undeniable. Educators like Ms. Dorris, Mr. Terry, Ms. Titus, Ms. Mjoen, and others highlighted in this book remind us that the real magic of education lies not in test scores or curriculum benchmarks, but in the connections forged and the lives transformed. It is never just about teaching facts or skills; it is about fostering hope, igniting curiosity, and creating ripples that could one day change the world.

Education is the cornerstone of progress and the foundation upon which all other professions are built. Without teachers, there would be no doctors, engineers, artists, or leaders. It is through education that societies develop, innovate, and thrive. While the influence of educators is often subtle, it is profound and enduring.

At its core, education is about empowerment. It equips individuals with the knowledge and skills they need to navigate an increasingly complex world. More than that, it instills values like curiosity, resilience, and critical thinking, shaping not only capable workers but thoughtful, informed citizens and people.

Consider the role of teachers in bridging gaps and breaking cycles. For many children, the classroom is a sanctuary - a place where they are seen, heard, and valued. It is often the first environment where they encounter opportunities to dream beyond their immediate circumstances. A teacher's encouragement can ignite ambitions that transform lives, lifting entire families out of poverty and creating a ripple effect that benefits communities for generations.

Education is also a powerful equalizer. It provides a pathway to opportunities that might otherwise be inaccessible, regardless of a person's background. A student's socioeconomic status, geographic location, or family circumstances need not dictate their future and often doesn't thanks to the dedication of educators who believe in their potential.

But education is more than a means to an end. It enriches the human experience, fostering creativity, empathy, and connection. Teachers are the architects of this enrichment. They inspire curiosity about the world, introduce students to diverse perspectives, and help them understand their place in a larger story.

To say that education is the most important job in the world is not hyperbole; it is an acknowledgment of its far-reaching impact. Educators, you remind us that education is not just a profession but a calling - one that holds the power to change lives, communities, and the world itself, so titles be damned; we implore you to begin learning, serving, and loving your students, colleagues, and in turn, our society.

Lead and Teach On, Beautiful, Tenacious Warriors; I'm rooting for you!

I have told the story many times of how I came to be an educator. It was not some noble calling; I wasn't the little kid who played school at home. No, I was not destined to be an educator. Rather, I was a kid who was a little lost, who really didn't have a path or a direction during their time in high school. Heck, I didn't have direction going into college. There was a moment for me, being asked to help coach a 5th grade girls basketball team; that helped me to discover my path. While this might be the origin of the story, the path continues to wind, to diverge, and to evolve in front of me. Along the way, I have learned a lot of lessons, met amazing people, and have built lifelong relationships that I genuinely cherish.

Among the biggest lessons taken away from nearly three decades as an educator, I would emphasize this: Culture matters. Relationships matter. People matter. You can have a great love of your subject matter as many do. You can enjoy coaching the sport, sponsoring the club, leading the band, or directing the play, as many of you do. That allows your passion to come out, to help fill that cup for you, and to pay forward your knowledge. But it all comes down to the fact that we are in the people business, and we cannot forget that.

I first discovered my Road to Awesome in a staff meeting many years ago. Honestly, I had no idea that day that something said in a quick, three second response would change me as a leader, as a father, as a human being, but it did. Two questions were asked that day. Picture this:
High school staff meeting
- Topics
    - Student behavior consequences
    - Hats - yes or no, consequences

- Cell phones - violations and consequences

You get the picture - and part way through the meeting, a hand was raised, and two questions asked. "Why does it always have to be about what they do wrong? Why can't it be about what they do right?"

This is what set me off on my Road to Awesome journey. No longer would I look for all the things our kids, or staff for that matter, were doing wrong. It was time to rethink how I was leading in my school.

When I first asked Katie to write this book with me, I wasn't entirely sure where we'd go with the content. I just knew that someone who had a similar passion as me about culture, about teachers, and about doing what is best for kids, we had to do something!

But this has become something bigger than just wanting to write with Katie which has been awesome. This is about a call to action. We've been in a funk for years shaking off the pandemic hangover, and it is time to reignite our love for school, our passion for kids, and to kickstart a classroom culture revolution. So many of you are doing it well, and I hope this book brought about ideas, thoughts, and inspiration. If you are new to the profession, start with your classroom culture in mind before anything else.

Being a culture first classroom means just that, put your culture first. Summarizing what we have discovered in the pages of this manuscript, being a culture first classroom means you focus on:

- what you can control
- building relationships
- being clear about your expectations, guidelines, and boundaries
- being strategic with room arrangement, procedures, and assessment
- creating a space where kids feel safe, welcome, and encouraged to grow and take risks
- leading from a place of love, compassion, understanding, and with a relentless belief in the ability of every child in your charge
- and never, ever, giving up

Being a culture first classroom is a movement, it's a calling, it's an opportunity. Seize the opportunity to be the very best you can be for those kids in your classroom, your school, and in your community.

And finally, thank you. You don't hear it often, certainly not enough, but thank you. The work you do is important, it makes an impact, and it cannot be done by just anyone. It takes a special human being with heart, grit, determination, maybe a little bit of crazy, patience, understanding, and a whole lot of love. Katie and I are not just colleagues and fellow educators, we are also parents. Parents of children who grew and developed through their public K-12 education. So, on behalf of parents everywhere, thank you.

ABOUT THE AUTHORS

Katie Kinder, author of *Untold Teaching Truths* and *Hallway Leadership*, is a highly sought after professional learning facilitator and speaker; she has been an educator since 2006. She brings her message of hope, fun, and real strategies to educators all over the nation. She believes that life is fun, and learning should most definitely be fun. Education Award Winner, Speaker, Author, Professional Development Leader, a Mom, a Wife, a Fierce Advocate for Education, and recognized nationwide for her distinctive teal glasses, Katie has learned a trick or two in the classroom, so come on in, have some fun, and hook your students from day one!

Dr. Darrin Peppard is a recovering high school principal, leadership coach, consultant, and speaker focused on organizational culture and climate and coaching emerging leaders.

Darrin is a best-selling author and is the host of the *Leaning into Leadership* podcast. He spent 26 years in public education, serving as a middle and high school teacher and coach in Kingman, Arizona for 11 years. He was then a high school assistant principal and principal in Rock Springs, Wyoming for 11 years. Darrin's final four years in public education were as the Superintendent of Schools in West Grand School District in Colorado. He was named the 2015 Jostens Renaissance National Educator of the Year and was the 2016 Wyoming Secondary School Principal of the Year. In 2019, Darrin was inducted into the Jostens Renaissance Educator Hall of Fame.

Darrin's work focuses on supporting emerging leaders and sharing the Road to Awesome message of culture, climate, and leadership. He is president and founder of Road to Awesome, LLC which provides coaching and consulting for leaders, inspirational keynote speeches for leaders of all walks of life, and publishes books by educators for educators. Darrin is also an adjunct professor in teacher education at Fort Hays State University (KS).

Darrin and his wife, Jessica, and daughter, Liz, currently live in Omaha, Nebraska. Darrin is a passionate but lousy golfer and enjoys time with family and in his Jeep.

MORE BOOKS BY ROAD TO AWESOME

Taking the Leap: A Field Guide for Aspiring School Leaders by Robert F. Breyer

Transform: Techy Notes to Make Learning Sticky by Debbie Tannenbaum

Becoming Principal: A Leadership Journey & The Story of School Community by Dr. Jeff Prickett

Elevate Your Vibe: Action Planning with Purpose by Lisa Toebben

#OwnYourEpic: Leadership Lessons in Owning Your Voice and Your Story by Dr. Jay Dostal

The Design Thinking, Entrepreneurial, Visionary Planning Leader: A Practical guide for Thriving in Ambiguity by Dr. Michael Nagler

Becoming the Change: Five Essential Elements to Being Your Best Self by Dan Wolfe

inspired: moments that matter by Melissa Wright

Foundations of Instructional Coaching: Impact People, Improve Instruction, Increase Success by Ashley Hubner

Out of the Trenches: Stories of Resilient Educators by Dana Goodier

Principled Leader
by Bobby Pollicino

Road to Awesome: The Journey of a Leader
by Darrin Peppard

When Calling Parents Isn't Your Calling: A teacher's guide to communicating with all parents
by Crystal Frommert

Struggle to Strength: Finding the Ingredients to Your Secret Sauce
by Kip Shubert

Guiding Transformational Change in Education
by Kristina V. Mattis

Be the Cause: An Educator's Guide to EFFECTive Instruction
by Josh Korb

Called to Empower
by Coach Kurt Hines

The Blueprint: Survive and Thrive as a School Administrator
by Todd M. Bloomer

Untold Teaching Truths
by Katie Kinder

Sustaining Excellence: How Culture Drives Teacher Retention
by Martin Silverman